ARKANA

Tao Te Ching

Richard Wilhelm lived in China for more than twenty years, coming into contact with some of the major Chinese intellectuals of the early twentieth century. Throughout his life he produced a steady stream of translations from Chinese, among the most notable being his translation of the *I Ching*, which is also published in the Arkana series.

TAO TE CHING
The Book of Meaning and Life

Lao Tzu

Translation and Commentary by
Richard Wilhelm

Translated into English by
H. G. Ostwald

ARKANA
PENGUIN BOOKS

ARKANA

Published by the Penguin Group
Penguin Books Ltd, 27 Wrights Lane, London W8 5TZ, England
Penguin Books USA Inc., 375 Hudson Street, New York, New York 10014, USA
Penguin Books Australia Ltd, Ringwood, Victoria, Australia
Penguin Books Canada Ltd, 10 Alcorn Avenue, Toronto, Ontario, Canada M4V 3B2
Penguin Books (NZ) Ltd, 182–190 Wairau Road, Auckland 10, New Zealand

Penguin Books Ltd, Registered Offices: Harmondsworth, Middlesex, England

First published in Great Britain as an Arkana Paperback by Routledge & Kegan Paul, 1985
Reprinted in Arkana 1990
5 7 9 10 8 6 4

German edition copyright © Eugen Diederichs Verlag GmbH & Co KG, Köln, 1978
This English translation copyright © Routledge & Kegan Paul, 1985
All rights reserved

Printed in England by Clays Ltd, St Ives plc

CONTENTS

PUBLISHER'S PREFACE
to the 1978 (German) edition

The Dao De Jing,* in its epigrammatic brevity, is a Book of Wisdom almost as inexhaustible as the DAO itself of which it treats. The forceful and immediate effect it still exercises upon us today, nearly three thousand years after it was first written, derives from the fact that Lao Zi gives expression to his insights in elemental – one is tempted to say archetypal – images.

Nevertheless, some knowledge of the cultural background from which the text evolved and drew its strength will be helpful for a more profound understanding of the work. What DAO means to Chinese culture, and what it can mean to us was set forth by Richard Wilhelm in his commentary 'The teaching of Lao Zi', first published in 1925. This commentary has been included in this new edition for the first time, as a valuable complement to the text.

*Publisher's note: It is now usual practice to transliterate Chinese into Pinyin – thus Lao Tzu becomes Lao Zi, *Tao Te Ching*, *Dao De Jing*, etc.. We have retained the more familiar forms on the cover.

For the sake of simplicity tone marks have been omitted throughout.

PREFACE

Experts in Chinese studies will agree that anyone undertaking a new translation of Lao Zi's *Dao De Jing* must put forward a good case for doing so. For no other Chinese literary text has attracted as much attention and as many attempts at translation in the past hundred years or so. The mysterious qualities and difficulties of the text are a challenge to thought and reflection. And as the *Dao De Jing* is a literary work which is not always understood even by Chinese scholars, the ambitious sinologue finds himself all the more tempted to undertake the task. For if many Chinese men of letters are not up to it, he feels he has a right – if he cannot do better – at least to misunderstand it. This justification for an individual interpretation may go even further still. It has been said that more than one uninhibited rendering of the ancient sage's work has been published that is based not on the Chinese text, but on an intuitive interpretation of what others – less inspired – had failed to grasp in terms of philosophical depth in their English or French versions of the text. Strangely enough, the psychological kinship often seems to be so close that the ancient Chinese sage will often show a remarkable sympathy with the thought of his respective translator.

In view of this profusion of translations, the reader may ask with good reason why yet another one should be added to their number. I have been encouraged to publish this new version for two reasons. The first constitutes the underlying principle of this edition. Among the many documents of Chinese religion and philosophy, this brief text, the source of so much influence, cannot be ignored – even if only the most important parts of it are to be represented, as is intended here. In addition, by placing the text in its true historical and philosophical context a new light will be cast on it, capable of clarifying and rectifying much that appears strange or incomprehensible when it is viewed in isolation. The second reason is that it seems a good idea that after so many modern interpretations the ancient Chinese sage himself should have his say.

The literature on Lao Zi is considerable. In working through it, I found the number of new things that have been said about him dismally small in proportion to the sheer quantity of what has been written. In fact, one discovers that certain common elements find their way from one book into all subsequent ones, partly by acknowledgment, and partly by rejection. Given this situation, there seemed to be no point in compiling yet another text from the existing ones: it seemed far more desirable to draw on Chinese literature itself. For this reason both the translation of the *Dao De Jing* and the commentary on the text are based on Chinese sources throughout.

At the same time, however, none of the more important issues in the continuing discussion of the *Dao De Jing* is thought to have been neglected. In certain circumstances even silence is a kind of recognition, particularly where the available space does not allow the translator to go into detail, and prove his own point of view. It is significant that new discoveries are made almost every day where Lao Zi is concerned, and it might have been tempting to offer yet another one. Instead, I have put forward many points here which may appear old-fashioned to some. Other questions which one would have liked to pronounce on decisively have had to be left unresolved. But that is how things are in this world: one cannot satisfy everybody.

On the whole I owe many happy hours of contemplation to my work on this brief Chinese text, and if this attempt at a new translation brings the same pleasure to its readers it will not have been in vain.

I want to thank Dr. jur. Harald Gutherz, lecturer at the law faculty of the new German-Chinese College at Qingdao who has generously contributed to this edition by permitting the inclusion of the fairy tale, stylised by him, in the commentary on section 80, and Friedrich Boie, schoolteacher at Thorn, who was kind enough to do the proof-reading.

Qingdao, 1 December 1910
Richard Wilhelm

INTRODUCTION

THE AUTHOR OF THE *DAO DE JING*

We know very little about the author of this collection of aphorisms in terms of historically established facts – so little, in fact, that Chinese scholarship has often been unable to find anything at all about him and has placed him and his work in the realm of mythology. Lao Zi himself, true to his nature, would hardly have objected to such treatment. He never attached any importance to fame, and knew well how to keep himself away from the world's gaze, both during his lifetime and after his death. The Chinese historian Si Ma Qian (163-85 BC) has this to say about him: 'He strove towards self-concealment and remaining without name'. We are indebted to Si Ma Qian for the essential data that we have on the author's life, and with these we have to make do.

The name Lao Zi under which he is known in Europe is not, in fact, a personal name but an epithet which is best translated as 'the Old One'.[1] His family name was Li, which is a very common name in China. In his youth he was called 'Er' ('ear'); as a scholar he was called 'Bo Yang' ('count Sun'); and after his death he was given the name 'Dan' or 'Lao Dan' (literally 'old long-ear', which means 'old teacher'). It seems that he came from what is now called the province of Henan, the southern-most of the so-called northern provinces. He was probably about fifty years older than Confucius, which would place his date of birth at the end of the seventh century BC.

During his lifetime he held the office of archivist at the Imperial Court, which was then at Luo-Yang, in what is now the

---

[1] The attempt to translate Lao Zi as the 'old philosophers' and thus to consider it a collective name for many sages of antiquity (H. Gipperich) is linguistically impossible. 'Lao' means *senex*, not *vetus*. The Chinese equivalent of *veteres* is *gu ren*.

province of Henan. It was at this time that Confucius is said to have met him, during his visit to the court. Much has been talked about this encounter between the two giants of Chinese letters. Apart from Si Ma Qian's historical work, their meeting is mentioned directly or indirectly in the book *Li Ji* which is of the Confucian school of thought, and in the rather late *Confucian School Tales, Jia Yu*, as well as in relatively early Daoist literature. In any case, this encounter had already become so much a part of popular consciousness by the time of the Han dynasty (second century BC), that we find an illustration of it among the famous tomb sculptures in western Chaodong (near Jia Xiang); here Confucius is depicted handing a pheasant to Lao Zi as a token of respect. There are a multitude of reports about the conversation which took place on this occasion. All are agreed that Lao Zi spoke in a rather deprecatory manner about Confucius's honoured idols, the heroes of ancient times, and that he tried to convince him of the futility of his cultural pursuits. Confucius, on the other hand, expressed his respect for the sage's unfathomable depths to his disciples – essentially by comparing him to the dragon who rises up to the clouds. The subject of the reported conversation can be gleaned to some extent from the pronouncements of the *Dao De Jing*, and from the tales about Confucius's encounter with the 'hidden sages' in *The Analects of Confucius*, book XVIII. It is obvious that nothing reliable can be gathered about the actual wording of their discourse. Whether one should judge the whole conversation as belonging to the realm of fiction – as Chavannes does in his translation of Si Ma Qian (*Les Mémoires historiques de Sé Ma Tsien*, vol. V, Paris, 1905, pp. 300ff.) – or not, it is difficult to decide. There is cause for concern in the fact that it was not actually reported in the *Analects*, although several other similar encounters are mentioned.[1]

Lao Zi is said to have left the court when political conditions had deteriorated so far that there was no longer any hope for a restoration of order. According to a later tradition, he arrived at

---

[1] Or is *Analects*, book XVIII, 5, a somewhat malicious polemic against the story of the encounter spread about by the Daoist side? In that case the passage could be indirect evidence. At any rate, the facts would have been forgotten later on because the commentaries do not refer to Lao Zi where they speak of 'the Fool of Chu' (Lao Zi is said to have come from Chu).

the provincial border at the mountain pass of Xian Gu, riding on the back of a black ox. The border official, Vin Xi, asked him to leave something in writing with him: at this request, Lao Zi wrote the *Dao De Jing* in 5,000 pictograms and gave it to him. He then went west, but nobody knows where. It is understandable that a further legend grew up around this tale, according to which Lao Zi went to India and got in touch with Buddha. In later disputations between Buddhism and Daoism, each side claimed that the founder of the other religion had learned from the founder of their own. In reality, however, the Xian Gu mountain is in the western part of what was then the state of Zhou, but no less in the heart of China. Any personal contact between Lao Zi and Buddha is completely out of the question: later conditions have been superimposed upon the historical picture.

But this was not the end of it. Just because the life of 'the Old One' offered so little to research, legends sprang up all the more freely. His personality reached gigantic proportions, and finally dissolved into a cosmic figure who was said to have appeared on earth at all kinds of times. The silly games played with the name Lao Zi (which can also be translated as 'old child') need not be dealt with in this context.

It follows quite clearly that we cannot learn much about Lao Zi's work from the fragmentary and uncertain facts of his life story. For the mystic, life histories – like all historical facts – dissolve into insubstantial apparitions. And yet: an original and inimitable personality speaks to us out of the aphorisms of the *Dao De Jing*. In our opinion this is the best proof of their historicity. But one must have the right kind of feeling for such things; there is no point in disputing them. In the end, the question is not of decisive importance. In any case: the *Dao De Jing* exists, no matter who wrote it.

THE TEXT

Chinese literature has paid far more attention to Lao Zi's work than to his personal life. At least one passage from the *Dao De Jing* is mentioned in *The Analects of Confucius* (book XVIII, 36). The possibility cannot be ruled out that this passage derives from earlier sources, which were accessible without reference to Lao Zi. But we are not exclusively dependent on this testimony.

In the first place one would have to look for quotations in Daoist literature. And indeed, there is no lack of these. We can establish that most of the eighty-one sections of the *Dao De Jing* have been quoted in the works of the most significant Daoist writers in pre-Christian times. For instance sixteen sections are cited by Lie Zi (whose text was published in the fourth century BC). Zhuang Zi (known as Tschuang Tse), the most brilliant Daoist writer who lived in the fourth century BC, based all of his writings on the teachings of the *Dao De Jing* – so much so that both he and his work are unthinkable without them. Han Fei Zi, who died in 230 BC under Qin Shi Huang Di, offers an elucidation of twenty-two sections which is often quite detailed, in books VI and VII. Finally, Huai-Nan-Zi, a contemporary of Si Ma Qian (he died in 120 BC) explains forty-one different sections in book XII, in sequence, mostly by means of historical examples. All in all, we have evidence of at least three-quarters of the available text in this form. For such a short work as the *Dao De Jing* these are rather favourable conditions. It also suggests that the *Dao De Jing* is not a Buddhist fake from later times, unless its origins can be traced to the 'big factory' of Si Ma Qian & Co., which Mr Allen had the honour of discovering.

During the Han dynasty several emperors took to studying the *Dao De Jing*, in particular Han Wen Di (179-157 BC), whose peaceful and simple way of government has been considered a direct result of the teaching of the old sage. His son Han Jing Di (156-140 BC) gave the book the title *Dao De Jing* ('the classical book of Meaning and Life') by which it has been known in China ever since. Han Wen Di is said to have received the book from He Shang Gong ('the Lord of the River'), who is also supposed to have written a commentary on it. Nothing definite is known about this man, whose real name nobody knows. Some Chinese authors (though of a later era) have even had doubts about his very existence. Yet from this time onwards, commentaries appear more frequently. In the catalogue of the Han dynasty alone three of them are mentioned. The oldest of the reliable commentaries which are still in existence is by Wang Bi, that marvellously gifted youth who died at the age of twenty-four in AD 249. After this, there have been ever-increasing numbers of commentaries of all kinds. Even the founder of the Manchu dynasty had a famous commentary published under his name.

It would be beyond the scope of this introduction to go into this in any more detail. There is no need to prove that a work like the *Dao De Jing* had much to suffer in the storms of ancient times, and that consequently the text is not at all in good condition. The notes on individual sections will deal with this in more detail.

Finally, the division of the text into sections is not authoritative. The division into two main parts, one called 'Meaning' (DAO), and the other 'Life' (DE), after the opening words of each part, does seem to be very old, however. These two words were later compounded to form the *Dao De Jing*. The present sub-division into two parts, the one containing 37 and the other 44 sections, [. . .] is said to go back to He Shang Gong.

HISTORICAL CONTEXT

The light of Chinese antiquity focuses on Confucius and Lao Zi. In order to appreciate their work fully and the effects they have produced, we must consider the historical circumstances in which they lived. This presents no difficulty where Confucius is concerned. He lived and worked amongst harsh realities, and can therefore be placed quite clearly in context. The *Analects*, for instance, are full of references to, and judgments upon, historical personalities of his own time and of the past. If one eliminated these relationships Confucius would be incomprehensible. It is precisely for this reason that he remains so utterly alien to European thought, with its different history, to this day; and on the other hand, this is the reason he had influenced Chinese thought so tremendously for two thousand years.

In Lao Zi's case, things seem to be very different. Not one historical name is mentioned anywhere in his brief text. He has no desire at all to influence what is temporal. As far as history is concerned, therefore, he fades into nebulous distance where no one may follow him. This is precisely the reason he has such a strong effect in Europe, in spite of the enormous distance in space and time that separates him from us.

The Japanese commentary by Dazai Shuntai gives an excellent description of the principles followed by the two men. He starts with a short review of contemporary historical conditions. According to his account Confucius looked upon the people as children who had drawn too close to the fire or the water, and therefore had to be rescued at any cost. He had realised how difficult the rescue would be, but this did not relieve him of the duty to rescue them. He had tried every means of applying the ancient saints' teachings, for he considered this to be the panacea. And so he had wandered about restlessly for the better part of his life, trying to find a prince willing to apply these teachings. It had not been shallow interference or vainglory that had driven him to these desperate efforts, but the inescapable duty to help because he knew he had the means to provide such help. And, finally, when all his efforts proved to be fruitless because conditons had deteriorated beyond repair, and circumstances did not help him at all, he resigned. Even then he did not forget his duty. He established a tradition amongst his disciples and through his literary work so that at least the outlines of the good, old social order might be saved for posterity, and his teachings be preserved as seed-corn for future times, so that – if more favourable circumstances should ever come about – there might be a means of setting the world to rights once again.

Lao Zi, however, had realised that the disease from which the realm was suffering was not one that could be cured by any – not even by the best – medicines. For the body of the nation was in a state that was fit for neither life nor death. Political conditions had been bad in earlier times, but then the evil had been embodied in some tyrant. The people had reacted angrily and forcefully by gathering around a noble reformer, and in this way had replaced the old order by a new and better one. But things were different in the time of the outgoing Zhou dynasty. Neither strong vices nor strong virtues prevailed. The people groaned under the oppression of their superiors, but did not have the strength for energetic action or for taking matters into their own hands. Their faults were not faults and their merits were not merits. A deep rooted inner falsehood had wormed its way into all relationships, so that although love of one's neighbour, justice and morals were still preached as high ideals, in fact greed and covetousness poisoned everything. Under these conditions, all attempts to put things right inevitably fuelled disorder. Such a disease could not be cured by external means.

It was better to let the diseased body rest so that it could recover ultimately with the help of Nature's own healing power. This was the meaning of the testament Lao Zi left behind in the 5,000 words of the *Dao De Jing*, when he left the world.

These gleanings from Dazai Shuntai's commentary sufficiently explain Lao Zi's weariness of the world of current affairs, and why there is not one historical example in his small book. In different rhythms and with different emphases, Rousseau preached the same truth in his 'return to Nature' in the mid-eighteenth century.

It would be wrong, however, to separate Lao Zi entirely from the context of Chinese spiritual life, for he is involved with it in thousands of ways. While it is true to say that history does not come within the orbit of his work, he did have a sound knowledge of Chinese antiquity: his work in the imperial archives gave him ample opportunity to familiarise himself with it. In his teaching he linked up with and had no reservations about using old adages of wisdom. His book is full of allusions; some are direct quotations, some – and probably most – are tacit references.

The fact that Lie Zi ascribes section 6 of the *Dao De Jing* to 'the Yellow Emperor', a mythical ruler from darkest antiquity, is itself an indication that many things that are written in the *Dao De Jing* have also been handed down elsewhere. Similarly, according to St Julien, Du Dao Jian traces all passages that begin 'Thus also the Man of Calling' to a book (*San*) *Fen* (*Wu*) *Dian*, and this, in turn, can be traced back to the same emperor. It would be difficult, if not impossible, to trace the origins of individual passages. Nor is this of any real significance, since such a strong homogeneous spirit pervades the whole work that everything in it has become the author's own, no matter when or where it originated.

We are satisfied with the fact that Lao Zi is as much part of a continuing tradition of ancient Chinese thought as Confucius. This is evident even from writings of the Confucian school. The concepts of DAO, which I have translated as 'Sinn', and of DE, which I have translated as 'Leben' ('Life'), are also given a great deal of prominence in Confucian writings: they are simply looked at in a different way. One can, in fact, often see the two schools carrying out a direct, mutual critique of one another. For instance, at the very beginning of the *Dao De Jing* there is a critique of the concept of the 'Way of the ancient kings' – the narrowly historical view of DAO commonly held by disciples of Confucius. The passage in Confucius's *Analects* which deals with Lao Zi's understanding of DE has already been mentioned. In some respects the two schools are in complete agreement with one another – for instance over the high value they both attribute to 'non-action' as a principle of government. But they are irreconcilably opposed over the value of *Li* (moral conduct and the rules that govern it): this is of cardinal importance to Confucius, while Lao Zi considers it a symptom of decadence and depravation. This has a great deal to do with Lao Zi's sceptical view of culture – in the sense of 'civilisation' –, on the one hand, and with the fact that he draws on older values than Confucius does, on the other; for Confucius deliberately identifies himself with the founders of the Zhou dynasty (cf. the *Feng Shen Yan Yi*) on this issue.

All this suggests that Lao Zi had at least as much spiritual affinity with ancient Chinese thought as Confucius had, and the latter seems to have remodelled tradition rather forcibly to suit his point of view. The fact that so much 'Daoist' thought can be found even in this remodelled material, in the *Book of Documents* (*Shu Jing*) as well as in the *Book of Changes* (*Yi Jing*) is the best evidence to support my case.

Lao Zi has shared the fate of other independent thinkers of all times, for while others took great pride in their 'glorious achievements' he often felt lonely in the current of contemporary life. But it seems that he did not find it too difficult to accept this fate. Unlike Confucius he did not found a 'school'. He neither needed nor wanted to do this, for he was not out to spread a doctrine. He looked into the great origins of the universe for himself, and with difficulty put into words what he had seen – leaving it to those of like mind in later times to consider his hints and suggestions, and discover for themselves the truths he had discovered. This he has achieved. In all times and ages there have been individual thinkers who have lifted their gaze beyond the passing phenomenality of human life, and up towards the eternal meaning of universal forces whose greatness surpasses all thinking. They no longer take the so-called 'seriousness' of life too seriously, for there is no essential value inherent in it. But these sages, too, were 'individuals apart'. It is implicit in this whole way of understanding life that it cannot be adhered to by the multitude. Nor did all these individuals possess the 'pure doctrine'. Each had his own way and made of it what he could – from Lie Yu Kou (Lie Zi) and Zhuang Zhou (Zhuang Zi), who have already been mentioned, to the 'Epicurean' Yang Zhu and the 'Philanthropist' Mo Di (Mo Zi) (the two scapegoats of the orthodox Confucian Meng Ke (Mencius)), to the sociologist Han Fei Zi, a contemporary of Qin Shi Huang Di, and Liu An (usually called Huai-Nan-Zi), the 'Romantic on the Throne' of Huai Nan.

But in later times as well, many of those who had battled bravely through life as faithful disciples of Confucius came to self-reflection as a result of the blows life had dealt them. They turned their backs on both the riches and pains of the world to find a quiet place in the mountains or by the sea, where they could seek the meaning of their experience of life in the *Dao De Jing*. One example may suffice for many.

There is a mountain range near Qing-Dao called Lao Shan, which is renowned in Chinese literature as the Island of the Blessed. Romantic rock formations and gorges enclose hidden monasteries; from their seclusion in copses of bamboo, almost buried in luxurious subtropical growth, they open up a view on to the wide blue sea. In this seclusion many a high official who had lost out in the bustle of warring factions at the imperial court, found peace in the contemplation of pure nature, and in reflection upon the sayings of the *Dao De Jing*. There is a description of the famous places in the Lao Shan – copies of which were only distributed among the monasteries – and I was lucky enough to obtain one such copy. It originates in those troubled times when the decaying Ming dynasty was displaced by the Manchu dynasty. An imperial censor made use of the unexpected leisure of his old age to take these notes. Almost every line shows the influence of 'the Old One'. The introduction itself begins with an exposition which reveals his spirit: 'A Being receives its value from being able to shine forth its own light, because it has touched the depths of the world's foundation. However, great art has no ornament, a great life does not shine, a great jewel has a rough outer appearance. How can these things make sense? Just through the recognition that the true light does not need to be acknowledged by men, that it is even almost ashamed of its brightness. The meaning of the good gifts of Heaven and Earth is not based on their usefulness for human purposes. One could even say that whatever does not have so much inner greatness that nothing more can be added to it from the outside does not deserve to be called great.'

But the effects of Lao Zi's teachings are not confined to China. The Japanese who has already been mentioned, said of himself: 'Even though I was born 2,000 years later, I have tried faithfully throughout my life to co-operate in bringing about the doctrines of Confucius. But it may be said that I overestimated my strength. Now I am nearly seventy years old and my days are rapidly drawing to an end. My will-power is still unbroken but my physical strength is ebbing away. Here I sit and watch how all things, all circumstances change, how everything deteriorates. Even if a Man of Calling were to stand up among us, he could no longer help. These are the same autumnal conditions which existed when Lao Dan wrote his 5,000 pictograms. In this time when everything is passing away, far better is the non-action of "the Old One" than the "Dao of the old kings".'

Some years ago, during a spiritualist seance in one of the Lao Shan monasteries, the 'Cave of the White Cloud' (Bai Yun Dong), a book was produced by means of that method of psychography which is fairly common in China, whereby the saints and sages of Chinese antiquity pronounce their teachings from beyond, one after another. The book is like all its companions. It contains much that is mysterious, much that is obscure, some passages of poetic splendour, but nothing of any value other than a kind of psychological interest. The words which the various ancient heroes pronounce to the disciples look fabulously like one another, and are always in complete agreement with the personal views of their seance-leader. One passage in the book is particularly amusing: 'But while Lao Zi was proclaiming his teachings' (with regard to which he appears to have remained remarkably consistent through the thousands of years that have passed since he wrote them), 'he suddenly interrupted himself and declared that he had just been called to London (Lun) in England (Ying), where they needed him; he would, in due course, return to continue his teaching.' Did the old priest in his remote mountain monastery which no European had yet reached, have a premonition that Lao Zi was becoming fashionable in Europe? However that may be, it is a fact that nowadays the threads that were first spun by Lao Zi are beginning to be woven into the cultural fabric of Europe. The most striking proof of this is Leo Tolstoy who acknowledges his relationship with Lao Zi, whom he greatly admired, in his doctrine of 'non-action'. And the multitude of translations of the *Dao De Jing* that are being published today are also a tribute to the hidden 'Old One'.

The reader may wonder why I have not yet mentioned the relationship between Lao Zi and Daoism, which one might think would be an obvious one. This omission is intentional: for Lao Zi is not the founder of today's Daoist religion. I am undeterred by the fact that the representatives of this religion worship him as God. There has, of course, never been a shortage of people since ancient times, and even in China itself, who have known how to project their own views into the *Dao De Jing* – whether they tried to combine its teaching with Confucianism, or found a tendency towards Buddhist contemplation in it; whether they sought its assistance in producing the elixir of life, or the philosopher's stone that turns lead into gold; or linked it into animistic polytheism or vegetarian or teetotal rites, or used the text to concoct spells for good or evil. This last cult even penetrated secret political groups, who tried to use ghostly spells at various times in order to overthrow the establishment. The old sage has had to lend his name to all and sundry. But all these cults and tendencies are, as a Chinese scholar correctly remarks, simply stealing from Lao Zi.

It is well known that the usual tripartite division of Chinese religion into Confucianism, Daoism and Buddhism is unsatisfactory and does not accurately represent reality. If one wanted to gain a true picture of Chinese religion one would first of all have to exclude Buddhism, which did not originate in China, and count it together with Islam and Christianity among foreign religions – even if it is the one foreign religion that has exercised the greatest influence on Chinese religious life. Second, Confucianism is not a religion but a social and political philosophy. It used the elements of existing religions as the bricks and mortar of its social system, selecting and screening these elements without really digesting them. It should be obvious from what has already been said that Lao Zi's Daoism has no church-forming capacity. What is nowadays commonly called Daoism is in fact derived from sources quite different from Lao Zi's *Dao De Jing*. It is nothing more than the animistic folk religion of ancient China, to some extent systematised, and interwoven with Indian lore. It is highly likely that this animistic folk religion – which probably took different forms in different regions, and only became a coherent system of beliefs as a result of the political unification of the various tribes – had existed already long before Lao Zi and Confucius; and this is borne out by certain passges in the *Analects* of Confucius. It has remained alive in the hearts of the nation to this day. This animism is a structure whose like can be found in deeper layers all over the world, in Christian Europe as well as in ancient Greece or in Israel. The only difference is that in Judaism and Christianity this animism is branded as a superstition. In China, however, it has led a relatively untroubled existence as something just good enough to keep the great masses in leash, while the educated reserve for themselves the privilege of treating it in whatever way their level of education or passing mood deems acceptable. This particular brand of Daoism is therefore no real challenge to Confucianism. Where there have been conflicts between the two, political power has always been the deciding factor. If one were to look for the heroes of this kind of Daoism – whose chief strength lies in exorcising spirits with all kinds of magic – one would have to mention Wei Bai Yang who lived during the time of the Han dynasty and who 'invented' the elixir of life; or Zhang Dao Ling (born AD 34) and Ken Kien Dschi (AD 423), who created the Daoist papacy under the title of Tian Shi ('Celestial Teacher') – an institution which still continues in hereditary form within the Zhang family, rather like the institution of the Dalai Lama which is carried on through metempsychosis. All this has nothing to do with Lao Zi, just as a benevolent fate has saved him from becoming a Daoist pope.

CONTENT

The metaphysics of the *Dao De Jing* is built on a foundation of intuition which cannot be formulated into static or narrowly defined concepts. Lao Zi 'painfully' called this DAO (see section 25 of the text). From the outset the correct translation of this word has been the subject of a great deal of controversy. 'God', 'Way', 'Reason', 'Word', 'Logos' (λογος) – these are just a few of the translations that have been suggested; while a number of writers have simply introduced the word 'Dao' into European languages without translating it. In point of fact, the term matters little since even for Lao Zi himself it was only a sort of algebraic symbol for something ineffable. It was for essentially aesthetic reasons that it seemed desirable to have a German word in a German translation. I have chosen to use the word 'Sinn' throughout.[1] I made this choice in the light of a passage in Goethe's *Faust* (Part I), in which Faust returns from his Easter outing, settles down to translate the New Testament and tries to render the opening words of the Gospel according to St John as 'Im Anfang war der Sinn'.[2] This would seem to be the translation that does most justice to the Chinese word DAO in its various meanings. The primary meaning of the Chinese word is 'way'; it then broadens out into meaning 'direction', 'state' (as condition) and from there into 'reason', 'truth'. Used as a verb the word means 'to speak', 'to say', or, metaphorically, 'to lead'. We do not need to consider the outside meanings of 'periphery/vicinity', or 'district' here. The German word 'Sinn' also has the original meaning of 'way', 'direction'. In addition, it implies: (1) 'the inner man's directedness towards something'; (2) 'the inner man as the seat of consciousness, perception, thinking, reflection' (cf. 'der innere Sinn', i.e. the intrinsic meaning); (3) 'bodily sensation', predominantly used in the plural ('die Sinne'); (4) 'meaning, idea, sense of words, images, actions' (see M. Heyne, *Deutsches Wörterbuch*, Leipzig, 1906). Among all these meanings only the one mentioned under (3) should be rejected as inapplicable to DAO; in other respects, though, the concurrence of meaning between the words 'Sinn' and DAO is very comprehensive. In order to emphasise the algebraic character of the word, it appears in capital letters throughout this translation.

The other term that occurs frequently in the *Dao De Jing* is DE. I have decided to translate this throughout, and to justify my decision give its Chinese definition: 'What beings receive in order to come about is called DE'. I have therefore translated the word as 'Life' (following John 1:4 : 'In him was life, and the life

---

[1] There is no single satisfactory English word for the German 'Sinn', as Wilhelm's encyclopedic definitions here suggest. I have therefore not attempted to translate it, but have retained the Chinese word DAO throughout this edition. ('Meaning' is as approximate a translation for 'Sinn', or 'Dao' as 'Word' is for 'Logos' in John, 1.) – *Trans.*

[2] Chinese translations of the Bible almost without exception, render 'Logos' as 'Dao'.

was the light of Man'). It would have been equally possible to translate it as 'nature', 'essence', 'spirit', 'power' – translations which have been used frequently in the *Analects* of Confucius; but I have avoided these here because they clash with other terms used in the text. The common rendering 'virtue' – which is more appropriate to later treatises on morals – suits Lao Zi even less than it suits Confucius.

After these introductory remarks on the two key terms in the *Dao De Jing*, I shall now go on to seek out the basic points on which Lao Zi founded his metaphysics. Immediately we have to establish an essential difference between his views and those of ancient Greek philosophy. The ancient Greek philosophers were outward-looking, and searched for a cosmological principle; it is no accident that a large number of their works are entitled: 'Peri physeos'. Nor is it surprising that as such a one-sided principle was pursued to its logical conclusion, its limitations had to become apparent at some point. In this respect, it does not make a great deal of difference whether one adopts 'water', 'fire', 'atoms', 'being' or 'spiritual matter' as the basic principle: all of these are only one aspect of a total experience, whose practical application is necessarily limited. This is why the individual philosophical systems of the cosmological era of Greek philosophy continuously changed and succeeded one another: for they all lacked a central foundation. It is also the reason that the main weakness of all these systems is revealed when they move into the realm of psychology. A system whose fundamental principle is cosmological cannot get beyond a materialistic psychology. As is well known, the *enantiodromia* of the Greeks developed through the subjectivist-sceptical era of the Sophists, and it was only in the third phase that the great systems of Democritus, Plato and, above all, Aristotle were created – systems which, by using all the material that had been worked over so often, prepared the way for a more unified philosophical approach.

Chinese thinking pursued an essentially different course. Neither Confucius nor Lao Zi ever strayed outside humanist territory. It is of the greatest importance to recognise this clearly, particularly where the teaching of Lao Zi is concerned. For although Confucius's orientation towards social ethics is hardly ever disputed, the DAO that Lao Zi speaks about may at first sight appear to be something purely cosmological. But this is only apparently so. Lao Zi repeatedly gives the departure point for his insights or, more adequately put, his views. For example, in section 21 he speaks of DAO and in section 54 of DE, or Life. In both instances he concludes with the question: 'Whence do I know that this is so?' – that is, what had just been claimed about DAO and DE. This question is followed by an answer that seems rather strange: 'Just through this.' In each case, the prominent position given to these words compels us to attribute a meaning to them which goes beyond the merely tautological. It is clear from the context in both sections that the insight is founded upon a general principle – which is also, however, present in the reflecting individual. It is precisely through this participation of the individual in the general principle of truth that these insights are assured of the source of all certainty: evidence.

If we now turn to a more practical consideration of Lao Zi's metaphysics, we notice that the following sentence occurs three times: ' "The Man of Calling" puts away the other and adheres to this' (sections 12, 38, 72). In time, every principle that has been derived from external experience will be disproved and become obsolete. For as mankind progresses man's knowledge of the world changes; and, in the end, the known world is the only existing 'world'. On the other hand, whatever is known from a central experience ('out of the inner light', as the mystics put it) will remain irrefutable, provided that it has been seen purely and truly. Therefore the harshest reproach that even Lao Zi's worst opponent, the cultural prophet Han Yu, could make was that the sage lived at the bottom of a well and did not see the world: but what he did see from there no man can refute. In this context it is useful to note that it is not the psychologically conditioned, accidental ego which is important to Lao Zi. The ego is the seat of illusion and danger. Lao Zi is concerned with the Self (the 'pure "I" ' which belongs to man-as-man). In order to progress from the empirical ego to this supra-individual entity a great deal of abstraction from everything accidental and distinctively individual is required. This penetration into the supra-individual sphere appears to be a decrease, while the business of research with its accumulation of individual, separate and specific insights appears as an increase (see section 48).

The most important thing is that the heart should become empty: only then can it comprehend the great truths. Lao Zi continually praises the empty heart as the ideal condition for true knowledge as well as for action. To understand this correctly we must not forget that for the Chinese the word 'heart' means something quite different from what it means in Christian-influenced, European thought. To a European the chief associations are with 'courage', or 'feelings' – and this colours and determines its meaning. For the Chinese, however, the word 'heart' primarily refers to one of the five senses; more specifically, it refers to that complex of senses which mediates most directly with the outside world, and which is commonly called 'sensation'. It follows from this that the heart is also the source of desire for external things. For Lao Zi all involvement with the empirical world through the senses and desires is perilous; it hinders true cognition because it is the source of illusion (see section 12). The way to penetrate to the truth consists in 'closing the gates' through which these illusionary impressions enter our inner world (cf. sections 52, 56). It is immediately obvious, then that all positive knowledge takes a back seat. In fact, Lao Zi dismisses all 'knowledge' and 'cognition' as insufficient (see sections 19, 20). One might think this would inevitably lead to a denial of the world. But this is not his intention at all. Instead his approach is based on the view that where appearances end, the true, hidden being – eternal, and superior to the fleeting changes of sensory illusion – comes into focus all the more clearly and purely. Lao Zi does not seek 'cognition' but 'seeing', inner 'enlightenment'. It is, however, made very clear in a number of places (see, for example, sections 3 and 12) that this 'seeing' has nothing to do with ascetic visions: on the contrary, Lao Zi absolutely approves of the care for one's 'body' and 'bones' necessary for one's physical well-being. This inner 'enlightenment' leads quite of its own accord to simplicity (see section 28), the most beautiful symbol of which is the child who has not yet been hurled about in the whirlpool of desires. The human being thus forms a continuous unity which returns into itself, and whose activity unfolds spontaneously. Within this unity, the expression of every principle or attribute is immediately complemented by its opposite, which is posited together with and by it, just as every wave in the sea is accompanied by a trough. This harmony of balance is not even disturbed by birth or death: for it brings with it eternal life, reaching beyond death.

At this point Lao Zi's consideration of the problem of

cognition leads him almost imperceptibly to a metaphysical principle: DE or Life. For according to Lao Zi Life is nothing other than this spontaneously active essence of man, identical, in the final analysis, with the foundation of the world. Spontaneity of activity is of the greatest importance in this respect: for this spontaneity is the secret of Life of the highest order (see section 38). From the point of view of the individual, however, this very spontaneity appears as something negative. For the individual 'holds back'. The individual does not live itself, but 'lets itself be lived', it is 'being lived' (see section 50). This is the reason that Lao Zi emphasises the principle of non-action. This non-action is not idleness or inertia, but a total receptiveness to that which wells up out of the metaphysical source in the individual. This is also the meaning conveyed by the various passages in the *Dao De Jing* which describe Life as female, as purely receptive. Life is 'good' in so far as it conducts itself 'adequately' at every moment and in every situation (see section 8). Its power consists precisely in offering the necessary complement in every relationship. It is good to the good, and to the non-good it is also good: for it gives to each its necessary complement. This complementarity is something that can be offered without conflict or strife; it is, in a manner of speaking, the filling of an empty space. But the act of offering this complementarity itself confers superiority on the giver. Therefore for Lao Zi 'good' is an alternating concept, one which cannot be established once and for all, but which has to be adapted to each individual case. Everything posited from a one-sided or single point of view is necessarily judged inferior. Even the highest virtue which defends and imposes itself is something inferior, because it represents only one side of the necessary pair of opposites. If everyone in the world recognises the good as good, then thereby the non-good is already posited. Therefore the Life that wants to impose itself by outward means, as a 'positive' force, is an inferior Life – even if it expresses itself as love of one's fellowmen, justice, or morality (see section 38). In every instance, a positive necessarily evokes a negative. Whoever identifies himself with only one side of such a pair of opposites thereby places himself in the wrong, considered from the highest point of view. Here we have the kind of view of life which underlies all tragedy – a view that has been particularly clearly formulated by Hebbel. Any step an individual takes beyond his individuality causes a reciprocal and balancing reaction from the universal continuum that has thus been disturbed.

The man who embodies this Life in himself, the ideal man, is called *Sheng Ren* throughout the *Dao De Jing*. I have translated this term as the 'Man of Calling'; though one can also find it translated as 'the saint'. The Man of Calling is the individual who, by putting away his individual inclinations and wishes, completely corresponds to the principle of Life. He does not live himself and does not seek anything for himself, but lets Life express itself through him. In this position he is, in a sense, a cosmic power. This is but a necessary consequence, for it is never possible to exclude man from the world, as he is always a necessary factor in that complex we call 'world'. (Even the most modern views of the world do not get beyond this point; after what Kant has shown us in his philosophical work it is no longer possible to have any serious doubts in this respect.) The 'Man of Calling' is, however, not realised in any historically specific personality. He is an idea beyond time, in some respects comparable to the idea of the Jewish Messiah, an idea in which everyone can participate according to his inner adaptation. (In this context, we might be able to throw some light on that obscure passage in section 4: 'I do not know whose son he is: he seems to be earlier than God.')

If we pursue 'spontaneity' a step further still, beyond the human realm, we come to DAO. Just as Life is spontaneity in man, so DAO is absolute spontaneity in the world. It is different from all things, it escapes all sensory perception. To this extent it does not come within the realm of existence either. Lao Zi repeatedly attributes the qualities of 'non-existence' or 'emptiness' to it. In order not to misunderstand these terms we should remember that the negative plays a part in Chinese philosophy that it does not play in European thought. For the Chinese, existence and non-existence are not contrary, not mutually contradictory opposites. The relationship of one to the other is like that of the negative and positive signs in mathematics. 'Nonexistence' is not purely a term of privation: it could, in fact, often be translated as 'being-by-' (or 'in') 'itself', in contrast to 'existence'. There are some interesting observations to be made with regard to the psychology of language, even in relation to modern colloquial Chinese. While it is possible to give double negation the value of 'strong positive' in Europe, the natural feeling of the language is usually quite against this kind of expression; in the Chinese language, however, it is quite common. Where we say 'He will definitely come', the Chinese have no hesitation in saying: 'He cannot not come'. They express 'omnipresence' as 'no place where he is not'. This complete equivalence between positive and negative is perhaps most clearly demonstrated in answers to negative questions. To the question 'Is he not coming?' a Chinese will answer 'Yes' if the person does not come, because the 'not' in the question does not signify negation for him: it combines with 'coming' into a compound concept, the concept of 'not-coming', and this can be confirmed without any risk of misunderstanding, just as any positive concept can.

Lao Zi's 'non-existence' must be understood in the same sense. It is not simply the same as nothingness, but something qualitatively different from existence. DAO is in all things but it is not itself a thing. Its effectiveness is essentially qualitative. An analogy can be found in the laws of nature. The laws of physics are expressed in all phenomena, but are not something distinct and separable, capable of interfering with the course of events from the outside. In the same way Lao Zi's DAO is present in all that happens: it can be left or right (see section 34) but it is not exhausted in anything that happens. This non-exhaustion or, as Lao Zi puts it, this 'non-filling-up', is the quality that makes it superior to all things, without this superiority ever expressing itself in any way. This non-expression of superiority, its 'weakness', can be called its 'smallness'; while its all-pervading effectiveness in all things accounts for its 'great-ness'.

Finally, it remains to be mentioned that the eternity of DAO rests on the fact that all of its movements 'return' into itself. All opposites are eliminated by it by being balanced against one another, so that every movement necessarily turns into its opposite. Once things have grown strong they die: it is just this strength, and the rigidity that goes with it, that brings about death. This principle is borne out by modern evolutionary theory, which shows how forms of life like that of the dinosaur gradually became extinct through developing too far and too inflexibly in one respect. Life always exists in the whole, never in isolation; therefore Nature does not know love as mankind does, but all things partake in its abundance: if men want to keep some of the affluence for themselves, they bring about their own death, just in this way.

From an ontological point of view, DAO is therefore the root of all existence: but since existence differs from non-existence only in name but not in essence, therefore DAO is also at work in existence. Here it is in the form of the motherly, the birth-giving which brings forth individual beings into life – and takes them back to itself in death.

Having ascended, by a process of induction, to Lao Zi's principle for explaining the world, we must now consider the opposite direction: the way in which he descends, deductively, from this highest principle to reality. As one might expect, it is here that he meets his greatest difficulties.

> The God who dwells within my breast
> Can deeply stir my inmost being.
> He who is enthroned on high above my strength,
> Cannot move a thing outside myself.
>
> Goethe, *Faust* (part I)

Lao Zi himself experienced some of the affliction that speaks from this verse, both personally, in relation to contemporary circumstances (as he laments in a tragic outburst – see section 20); and in tracing the course of the external world from DAO. However, he cannot really be reproached for this, for there remains an irrational residue in the effective which cannot be grasped by thought alone. Perhaps it is precisely this irrational residue that is the ground of every individual's existence. Since time immemorial, mankind has chafed against this without finding an answer to questions which perhaps cannot be resolved at all, except by the will of the individual, for the individual. We must not expect Lao Zi to succeed where no other philosopher has succeeded before or since – in other words, in penetrating to reality ('to that which is the effective') by means of thought alone. Nevertheless, the lines that Lao Zi draws to indicate the direction in which DAO moves towards the real (the effective), are of great interest. There are two central issues to be considered here: on the one hand the movement that leads from DAO, as the final unity, to the coming about of the manifold; and on the other the lines that point from thought to reality. The principle of unity is the basis of Lao Zi's philosophy. In this respect, he is decidedly a monist (just as, incidentally, all Chinese thinking is fundamentally monist – in spite of the prominence given to teachings about dual powers, for these are at work only within the world, that is, not transcendentally). This unity is the ultimate point to which all thought ascends, the secret of secrets, the gateway to the revelation of all powers (see section 1). Within this unity all opposites are still intermingled with one another, as yet unseparated. It is that which is usually called 'non-existence' which lies even before the 'primal beginning' (see note to section 1, at the end of this edition). The One, as thesis, generates the Two, as antithesis (the opposites of light and dark, male and female, positive and negative, for example). From these pairs of opposites the visible world is born as the Three.

The progression from unity to multiplicity – without thereby creating something completely different – is made possible by the fact that multiplicity is already inherent in unity, although it cannot as yet be seen in its germinal state. This is probably the meaning of section 14, where it is said that inherent in DAO are an invisible visibility, an inaudible audibility and an impalpable palpability; and that these three are inextricably intermingled and form one. This multiplicity in unity makes further unfolding, further development, possible. It is immediately obvious that this is not the result of the creation of the world at a specific historical time. For this unfolding is an essentially logical process, which can indeed be projected back in time and called the beginning of Heaven and Earth; but it shows itself equally within the spatial world, in the continuous regeneration of life (see section 1). Unity unfolded into multiplicity is also mentioned in section 25, where this unfolding is represented as a circular movement. DAO reveals itself in a perpetual state of flux: it works in Heaven, that is in the totality of invisible, effective, non-material forces; and, emanating from there, it overflows into the most distant places, fructifying the Earth, or the totality of material corporeality; and finally, it returns to itself in man. Accordingly, Man, Earth and Heaven are always prefigured in the nearest preceding level of Existence. Their *modus operandi* is thus derived from DAO, which alone has immediate effect. This unity is identified in section 39 of the *Dao De Jing* as the root source of the directedness of Heaven, Earth, and Man as ruler. (In this particular section there are two additional complexes of ideas, 'the gods' and 'the valley', which I shall discuss in more detail below.)

The transition from DAO to reality must be distinguished from the relationship between unity and multiplicity. In this respect sections 14 and 21, and the beginning of section 51 are of particular significance. Here we find hints as to how reality is potentially inherent in DAO. Any attempt to systematise these individual intuitions, which elude conceptual expression, would be doomed to failure. These passages are the hesitant expressions of experiences which transcend human thought. One could say that there is a certain kinship between Lao Zi's views and Plato's teaching on ideas. In these passages the point is often made that the effectiveness of DAO within individual beings in reality is possible precisely because formless, non-corporeal ideas or images are contained in it in a way that is beyond comprehension. In order to communicate these ideas Lao Zi uses on the one hand, the concept of Life: 'the content of the great Life completely follows DAO', that is, shapes itself according to it (see section 21); and on the other, the concept of 'the seed'. I have already spoken about the relationship between Life and DAO in this Introduction. The concept of the seed takes up a position between the world of ideas and the corporeal-material world. According to section 21, the seed partakes of reality: in this way the connection with the external world is established. In addition to these concepts, Lao Zi uses the more commonly held conception of the duality of Heaven and Earth. Heaven, in this context, represents the spiritual powers; Earth stands nearer to the material world, the greatest degree of self-effacement of DAO. Another pair of concepts which appear in sections 6 and 39 should also be mentioned here: 'the deep' or 'emptiness' (literally 'the valley'); and 'the spirit' or 'the gods' (*Shen*). 'The deep' or 'emptiness' originally referred to 'the space between two mountain slopes'. It has come to mean 'life as it is formed through the action of the spirit': this is probably bound up with even earlier mythical representations. In this way 'the deep' has almost paradoxically come to mean what we call 'matter', that is, the as yet undefined, inactive, sheer possibility of existence; 'spirit' provides the corresponding active principle. It would lead beyond the limits of this introduction to follow these hints and suggestions to their conclusion. We would almost certainly find ourselves involved in a chain of ideas which would deviate to some extent from those pursued in the *Dao De Jing*. I mention them here, however, in order to draw attention to them.

Later Daoism has conducted some far-reaching speculations along these lines. Some of these have led to extravagant fantasies about alchemical attempts to find an elixir of life, or redeem the body from mortality through physical exercise. It is a measure of the height of Lao Zi's own standpoint that these things are alien to him, and that he restricts himself to hints at the ineffable, the pursuit of which is left to the individual.

THE DAO DE JING

Part I
DAO

1

The DAO that can be expressed
is not the eternal DAO.
The name that can be named
is not the eternal name.
'non-existence' I call the beginning of Heaven and Earth.
'Existence' I call the mother of individual beings.
Therefore does the direction towards non-existence
lead to the sight of the miraculous essence,
the direction towards existence
to the sight of spatial limitations.
Both are one in origin
and different only in name.
In its unity it is called the secret.
The secret's still deeper secret
is the gateway through which all miracles emerge.

2

If all on earth acknowledge the beautiful as beautiful
then thereby the ugly is already posited.
If all on earth acknowledge the good as good
then thereby is the non-good already posited.
For existence and non-existence generate each other.
Heavy and light complete each other.
Long and Short shape each other.
High and deep convert each other.
Before and after follow each other.

Thus also is the Man of Calling.
He dwells in effectiveness without action.
He practises teaching without talking.
All beings emerge
and he does not refuse himself to them.
He generates and yet possesses nothing.
He is effective and keeps nothing.
When the work is done

he does not dwell with it.
And just because he does not dwell
he remains undeserted.

3

By not preferring the competent
one brings about that people do not quarrel.
By not treasuring precious things
one brings about that people do not steal.
By not displaying desirable things
one brings about that people's hearts are not confused.

Therefore the Man of Calling governs thus:
He empties their hearts and fills their bellies.
He weakens their will and strengthens their bones
and brings about that the people remain without knowledge
and without wishes,
and he takes care
that those who know dare not act.
He does the non-doing,
and thus everything falls into place.

4

DAO is forever flowing.
And yet it never overflows in its effectiveness.
It is an abyss like the ancestor of all things.
It mellows their acuity.
It dissolves their confusion.
It mitigates their brightness.
It unites itself with their dust.
It is deep and yet as if real.
I do not know whose son it is:
It seems to be earlier than God.

5

Heaven and Earth are not benevolent.
To them men are like straw dogs destined for sacrifice.
The Man of Calling is not benevolent.

To him men are like straw dogs destined for sacrifice.
The space between Heaven and Earth
is like a flute:
empty, and yet it does not collapse;
when moved more and more emerges from it.
But many words exhaust themselves on it.
It is better to guard the 'within'.

6

The spirit of the valley never dies.
It is called 'the female'.
The gateway of the dark female
is called 'the root of Heaven and Earth'.
Uninterrupted as though persistent
it is effective without effort.

7

Heaven is eternal and Earth lasting.
They are lasting and eternal
because they do not live for themselves.
Therefore can they live forever.

Thus also is the Man of Calling:
He disregards himself,
and his Self is increased.
He gives himself away
and his Self is preserved.
Is it not thus:
because he desires nothing as his own
his own is completed?

8

The highest benevolence is like water.
The benevolence of water is
to benefit all beings without strife.
It dwells in places which man despises.
Therefore it stands close to DAO.
In dwelling benevolence shows itself in place.

In thinking benevolence shows itself in depth.
In giving benevolence shows itself in love.
In speech benevolence shows itself in truth.
In ruling benevolence shows itself in order.
In working benevolence shows itself in competence.
In movement benevolence shows itself in timing.
He who does not assert himself
thereby remains free of blame.

9

To hold on to something and thereby make it overflow:
this is not worthwhile.
To make use of something and still keep it sharp:
this cannot be sustained for long.
A palace full of gold and diamonds
nobody can protect.
To be rich and titled and arrogant into the bargain:
this in itself attracts misfortune.
When the work is done it is time to withdraw:
this is the DAO of Heaven.

10

Can you educate your soul so that it encompasses the One
without dispersing itself?
Can you make your strength unitary
and achieve that softness
that makes you like a little child?
Can you cleanse your secret seeing
so that it becomes free of stain?
Can you love men and rule the state
so that you remain without knowledge?
Can you, when the gates of Heaven
open and close, be like the female bird?
Can you penetrate everything with your inner clarity and purity
without having need for action?
Generating and nourishing,
generating and not possessing,
being effective and not retaining,
increasing and not dominating: this is the secret Life.

11

Thirty spokes surround the hub:
In their nothingness consists the carriage's effectiveness.
One hollows the clay and shapes it into pots:
In its nothingness consists the pot's effectiveness.
One cuts out doors and windows to make the chamber:
In their nothingness consists the chamber's effectiveness.

Therefore: what exists serves for possession.
What does not exist serves for effectiveness.

12

The five colours blind men's eyes.
The five tones deafen men's ears.
The five flavours spoil men's palates.
Running and chasing make men's hearts mad.
Rare goods confuse men's ways.

Therefore the Man of Calling
works for the body's needs, not for the eye's.
He removes the other and takes this.

13

Grace is as shameful as a fright.
Honour is a great evil like the persona.
What does this mean: 'Grace is as shameful as a fright'?
Grace is something inferior.
One attains it, and one is as if frightened.
This is what is meant by 'Grace is as shameful as a fright'.
What does this mean: 'Honour is a great evil like the persona'?
The reason I experience great evil is
that I have a persona.
If I have no persona:
What evil could I experience?

Therefore: whosoever honours the world in his persona
to him one may entrust the world.
Whosoever loves the world in his persona
To him one may hand over the world.

14

One looks for it and does not see it:
its name is 'seed'.
One listens for it and does not hear it:
its name is 'subtle'.
One reaches for it and does not feel it:
its name is 'small'.
These three cannot be separated,
therefore, intermingled they form the One.
Its highest is not light,
its lowest is not dark.
Welling up without interruption,
one cannot name it.
It returns again to non-existence.
This is called the formless form,
the objectless image.
This is called the darkly chaotic.
Walking towards it one does not see its face;
following it one does not see its back.
If one holds fast to the DAO of antiquity
in order to master today's existence
one may know the ancient beginning.
This means: DAO's continuous thread.

15

Those who in ancient times were competent as Masters
were one with the invisible forces of the hidden.
They were deep so that one cannot know them.
Because one cannot know them
therefore one can only painfully describe their exterior.
Hesitating, like one who crosses a river in winter,
cautious, like one who fears neighbours on all sides,
reluctant, like guests,
dissolving like ice that is melting,
simple like unworked matter:
broad they were, like the valley,
impenetrable to the eye they were like the turbid.
Who can clear up the turbid, little by little,
through stillness (as they did)?

Who can create stillness, little by little,
through duration (as they did)?
Whosoever guards this DAO
does not desire abundance.
For only because he has no abundance
therefore can he be modest,
avoid what is new
and attain completion.

16

Create emptiness up to the highest!
Guard stillness up to the most complete.
Then all things may rise together.
I see how they return.
Things in all their multitude:
each one returns to its root.
Return to the root means stillness.
Stillness means return to fate.
Return to fate means eternity.
Cognition of eternity means clarity.
If one does not recognise the eternal
one falls into confusion and sin.
If one recognises the eternal
one becomes forbearing.
Forbearance leads to justice.
Justice leads to mastery.
Mastery leads to Heaven.
Heaven leads to DAO.
DAO leads to duration.
All one's life long one is not in danger.

17

If a wholly Great One rules
the people hardly know that he exists.
Lesser men are loved and praised,
still lesser ones are feared,
still lesser ones are despised.
How thoughtful one must be in what one says!
The work done, business takes its course,

and all people think:
'We are free.'

18

If the great DAO perishes
there will be morality and duty.
When cleverness and knowledge arise
great lies will flourish.
When relatives fall out with one another
there will be filial duty and love.
When states are in confusion
there will be faithful servants.

19

Put away holiness, throw away knowledge:
thus the people will profit a hundredfold.
Put away morality, throw away duty:
thus the people will return to filial duty and love.
Put away skilfulness, throw away gain,
and there will no longer be thieves and robbers.
In these three things
beautiful appearance is not enough.
Therefore take care that men have something to hold on to.
Show simplicity, hold fast to honesty!
Diminish selfishness, reduce desire!
Give up learnedness!
Thus you shall become free of sorrows.

20

Between 'definitely' and 'probably':
what difference is there?
Between 'good' and 'evil':
what difference is there?
What men honour one must honour.
O loneliness, how long will you last?
All men are so shining-bright
as if they were going to the great sacrificial feast,
as if they were climbing up the towers in spring.

Only I am so reluctant, I have not yet been given a sign:
like an infant, yet unable to laugh;
unquiet, roving as if I had no home.
All men have abundance,
only I am as if forgotten.
I have the heart of a fool: so confused, so dark.
Men of the world are shining, alas, so shining-bright;
only I am as if turbid.
Men of the world are so clever, alas, so clever;
only I am as if locked into myself,
unquiet, alas, like the sea,
turbulent, alas, unceasingly.
All men have their purpose,
only I am futile like a beggar.
I alone am different from all men:
But I consider it worthy
to seek nourishment from the Mother.

21

The substance of the great Life
completely follows DAO.
DAO brings about all things
so chaotically, so darkly.
Chaotic and dark
are its images.
Unfathomable and obscure in it
is the seed.
This seed is wholly true.
In it dwells reliability.
From ancient times to this day
we cannot make do without names
in order to view all things.
Whence do I know the nature of things?
Just through them.

22

What is half shall become whole.
What is crooked shall become straight.
What is empty shall become full.

What is old shall become new.
Whosoever has little shall receive.
Whosoever has much, from him shall be taken away.

Thus also is the Man of Calling:
he encompasses the One
and sets an example to the world.
He does not want to shine,
therefore will he be enlightened.
He does not want to be anything for himself,
therefore he becomes resplendent.
He does not lay claim to glory,
therefore he accomplishes works.
He does not seek excellence,
therefore he will be exalted.
Because whosoever does not quarrel
with him no-one in the world can quarrel.
What the ancients said: 'That which is half shall become full,'
is truly not an empty phrase.
All true completeness is summed up in it.

23

Use words sparingly,
then all things will fall into place.
A whirlwind does not last a whole morning.
A downpour of rain does not last a whole day.
And who works these?
Heaven and Earth.
What Heaven and Earth cannot do enduringly:
how much less can man do it?

Therefore if you set about your work with DAO
you will be at one in DAO with those who have DAO,
at one in Life with those who have Life,
at one in poverty with those who are poor.
If you are at one with them in DAO
those who have DAO will come to meet you joyfully.
If you are at one with them in Life
those who have Life will come to meet you joyfully.
If you are at one with them in poverty

those who are poor will come to meet you joyfully.
But where faith is not strong enough
there one is not believed.

24

Whosoever stands on tiptoe
does not stand firmly.
Whosoever stands with legs astride
will not advance.
Whosoever wants to shine
will not be enlightened.
Whosoever wants to be someone
will not become resplendent.
Whosoever glorifies himself
does not accomplish works.
Whosoever boasts of himself
will not be exalted.
For DAO he is like kitchen refuse and a festering sore.
And all the creatures loathe him.
Therefore: whosoever has DAO
does not linger with these.

25

There is one thing that is invariably complete.
Before Heaven and Earth were, it is already there:
so still, so lonely.
Alone it stands and does not change.
It turns in a circle and does not endanger itself.
One may call it 'the Mother of the World'.
I do not know its name.
I call it DAO.
Painfully giving it a name
I call it 'great'.
Great: that means 'always in motion'.
'Always in motion' means 'far away'.
'Far away' means 'returning'.
Thus DAO is great, Heaven is great, Earth is great,
and Man too is great.
There are in space four Great Ones,

and Man is one of them.
Man conforms to Earth.
Earth conforms to Heaven.
Heaven conforms to DAO.
DAO conforms to itself.

26

The weighty is the root of the light.
Stillness is the lord of restlessness.

Thus also is the Man of Calling.
He wanders all day
without discarding his heavy load.
Even when he has all the glory before his eyes
he remains satisfied in his loneliness.
How much less may the lord of the realm
take the world lightly in his persona!
By taking it lightly one loses the root.
Through restlessness one loses mastery.

27

A good wanderer leaves no trace.
A good speaker has no need to refute.
A good arithmetician needs no abacus.
A good guard needs neither lock nor key –
and yet no-one can open what he guards.
A good binder needs neither string nor ribbon,
and yet non-one can untie what he has bound.
The Man of Calling always knows how to rescue men:
therefore, for him there are no abject men.
He always knows how to rescue things:
therefore for him there are no abject things
This means: living in clarity.
Thus good men are the teachers of the non-good,
and non-good men are the subject-matter of the good.
Whosoever does not cherish his teachers
and does not love his subject-matter:
for all his knowledge he would be in grave error.
This is the great secret.

28

Whosoever knows his maleness
and guards his femaleness:
he is the gorge of the world.
If he is the gorge of the world
eternal Life does not leave him
and he becomes again as a child.

Whosoever knows his purity
and guards his weakness
is an example to the world.
If he is an example to the world
eternal Life does not leave him
and he returns to the uncreated.

Whosoever knows his honour
and guards his shame:
he is the valley of the world.
If he is the valley of the world
he finds satisfaction in eternal Life
and returns to simplicity.

If simplicity is dispersed there will be 'useful' men.
If the Man of Calling practises it
he will be the lord of the servants.
Therefore: Great Design
has no need for pruning.

29

Conquering and handling the world:
I have experienced that this fails.
The world is a spiritual thing
which must not be handled.
Whosoever handles it destroys it,
whosoever wants to hold on to it loses it.
Now things run ahead, now they follow.
Now they blow warm, now they blow cold.
Now they are strong, now they are thin.
Now they are on top, now they topple.

Therefore the Man of Calling avoids
what is too intense, too much, too big.

30

Whosoever in true DAO helps a ruler of men
does not rape the world by use of arms,
for actions return onto one's own head.
Where armies have dwelt thistles and thorns grow.
Behind battles follow years of hunger.
Therefore the competent seeks only decision, nothing further.
He does not dare conquer by force.
Decision without boasting;
decision without glorifying;
decision without arrogance;
decision because it cannot be helped;
decision removed from force.

31

Weapons are instruments of bad omen:
all beings, I believe, loathe them.
Therefore, whosoever has the true DAO
does not want to know about them.
The noble man, in his ordinary life,
considers the left the place of honour.
In the art of warfare
the right is the place of honour.
Weapons are instruments of bad omen,
not instruments for the noble.
He uses them only when he cannot help it.
Quietness and peace are his highest values.
He gains victory but he does not rejoice in it.
Whosoever would rejoice in it
would, in fact, rejoice in the murder of men.
Whosoever would rejoice in the murder of men
cannot achieve his goal in the world.
In fortunate circumstances one considers the left the place of
 honour.
In unfortunate circumstances one considers the right the place of
 honour.

The vice-commander stands to the left,
the supreme commander to the right.
This means: he takes his place
according to the rules for memorial services.
Killing men in great numbers
one must bewail with tears of compassion.
Whosoever has been victorious in battle
shall linger as if attending a memorial service.

32

DAO as the eternal is unutterable simplicity.
Even though it is small
the world dares not make it its serf.
If princes and kings could guard it in this manner
all things would come to be their guests.
Heaven and Earth would unite
to shed sweet dew.
People would find their balance
all by themselves, without orders.
When creation begins,
only then are there names.
Names too reach existence,
and one still knows where to halt.
If one knows where to halt
one is in no danger.
The relation between DAO and world
may be compared
to mountain streams and valley brooks,
that shed themselves into rivers and seas.

33

Whosoever knows others is clever.
Whosoever knows himself is wise.
Whosoever conquers others has force.
Whosoever conquers himself is strong.
Whosoever asserts himself has will-power.
Whosoever is self-sufficient is rich.
Whosoever does not lose his place has duration.
Whosoever does not perish in death lives.

34

The great DAO is overflowing:
it can be to the left and to the right.
All things owe their existence to it,
and it does not refuse itself to them.
When the work is done it does not call it its possession.
It clothes and nourishes all things
and does not play at being their master.
Inasmuch as it is forever not clamouring
one may call it small.
Inasmuch as all things depend on it
without knowing it as its master
one may call it great.

Thus also is the Man of Calling:
He never makes himself look great:
therefore he achieves the great work.

35

Whosoever holds fast to the great primal image,
to him the world will come.
It comes and is not violated:
In calmness, equity and blessedness.

Music and allurement:
They may well make the wanderer stop in his tracks.
DAO issues from the mouth,
mild and without taste.
You look for it and you see nothing special.
You listen for it and you hear nothing special.
You act according to it and you find no end.

36

What you want to compress
you must first allow truly to expand.
What you want to weaken
you must first allow to grow truly strong.
What you want to destroy

you must first allow truly to flourish.
From whomever you want to take away
to him you must first truly give.
This is called 'being clear about the invisible'.
The soft wins victory over the hard.
The weak wins victory over the strong.
One must not take the fish from the deep.
One must not show the people
the means of furthering the realm.

37

DAO is eternal without doing,
and yet nothing remains not done.
If princes and kings know how to guard it
all things will take shape by themselves.
If they take shape by themselves and desires arise
I should banish them with unutterable simplicity.
Unutterable simplicity works departure of desire.
Being without desire makes still,
and the world rights itself.

Part II
DE, or LIFE

38

Whosoever cherishes Life
does not know about Life
therefore he has Life.
Whosoever does not cherish Life
seeks not to lose Life:
therefore he has no Life.
Whosoever cherishes Life
does not act and has no designs.
Whosoever does not cherish Life
acts and has designs.
Whosoever cherishes love acts but has no designs.
Whosoever cherishes justice acts and has designs.
Whosoever cherishes morality acts
and if someone does not respond to him
he waves his arms about and pulls him up.
Therefore: If DAO is lost, then Life.
If love is lost, then justice.
If justice is lost, then morality.
Morality is the penury of faith and trust
and the beginning of confusion.
Foreknowledge is the sham of DAO
and the beginning of folly.
Therefore the right man abides with fullness
and not with penury.
He lives in being, not in sham.
He puts the other away and adheres to this.

39

Those of old who attained the One:

Heaven attained the One and became pure.
Earth attained the One and became firm.
The Gods attained the One and became powerful.
The valley attained the One and fulfilled itself.
All things attained the One and came into existence.

Kings and princes attained the One
and became examples to the world.
All this has been effected by the One.
If Heaven were not pure through it, it would have to burst.
If Earth were not firm through it, it would have to falter.
If the gods were not powerful through it
they would have to become rigid.
If the valley were not fulfilled through it,
it would have to exhaust itself.
If things had not come into existence through it,
they would have to perish.
If kings and princes were not exalted by it,
they would have to tumble.
Therefore: The noble has the lowly for its root.
The high has the low for its foundation.

Therefore princes and kings are thus:
They call themselves 'lonely', 'orphaned', 'trifling'.
Through this they name the lowly as their root.
Is it not so?

For: without its individual parts
there is no carriage.
Do not desire the glitter of the jewel
but the raw roughness of the stone.

40

Return is the movement of DAO.
Weakness is the effect of DAO.
All things under Heaven come about in existence.
Existence comes about in non-existence.

41

If a sage of the highest order hears about DAO
he is keen to act in accordance with it.
If a sage of the middle order hears about DAO
he half believes and half doubts.
If a sage of the lower order hears about DAO
he laughs loudly about it.

If he does not laugh loudly
then it was not yet the true DAO.

Therefore the poet has these words:
'The clear DAO appears to be dark.
The DAO of progress appears as retreat.
The smooth DAO appears to be rough.
The highest Life appears as a valley.
The highest purity appears as shame.
The broad Life appears to be insufficient.
The strong Life appears to be stealthy.
The true essence appears to be changeable.
The great quadrant has no corners.
The great instrument is completed late.
The great tone has an inaudible sound.
The great image has no form.'

DAO in its seclusion has no name.
And yet it is precisely DAO
that is good at giving and completing.

42

DAO generates the One.
The One generates the Two.
The Two generates the Three.
The Three generates all things.
All things have darkness at their back
and strive towards the light,
and the flowing power gives them harmony.

What men hate
is forlornness, loneliness, being a trifle.
And yet, princes and kings
choose these to describe themselves.
For things are either increased through diminution or
diminished through increase.
I, too, teach what others teach:
'The strong do not die a natural death'.
This I will make the departure point of my teaching.

43

The softest thing on earth
overtakes the hardest thing on earth.
The non-existent overtakes even that
which has no interstices.
From this one recognises the value of non-action.
Teaching without words, the value of non-action
is attained by but few on earth.

44

Name or person:
which is closer?
Person or possession:
which is more?
Winning or losing:
which is worse?

But then:
whosoever hankers after other things
inevitably uses up the great things.
Whosoever amasses things
inevitably loses the important things.
Whosoever is self-sufficient
does not come to shame.
Whosoever knows how to practise restraint
does not get into danger
and thus can last forever.

45

Great completion must appear as if inadequate:
thus it becomes infinite in its effect.
Great abundance must appear as if flowing:
thus it becomes inexhaustible in its effect.
Great straightness must appear as if crooked.
Great talent must appear as if foolish.
Movement overcomes cold.
Stillness overcomes heat.
Purity and stillness are the world's measuring gauge.

46

When DAO rules on earth
one uses the racehorses to pull dung carts.
When DAO has been lost on earth
warhorses are raised on the green fields.
There is no greater sin than many desires.
There is no greater evil than not to know sufficiency.
There is no greater defect than wanting to possess.

Therefore: the sufficiency of sufficiency is lasting sufficiency.

47

Without going outdoors
one knows the world.
Without looking out of the window
one sees the DAO of Heaven.
The further out one goes
the lesser one's knowledge becomes.

Therefore, the Man of Calling does not need to go
and yet he knows everything.
He does not need to see
and yet is he clear.
He does not need to do anything
and yet he completes.

48

Whosoever practises learning increases daily.
Whosoever practises DAO decreases daily.
He decreases and decreases
until at last he arrives at non-action.
In non-action nothing remains not done.
The realm can only be attained
if one remains free of busy-ness.
The busy are not fit
to attain the realm.

49

The Man of Calling has no heart of his own.
He makes the people's heart his own heart.
'To the good I am good;
to the non-good I am also good,
for Life is goodness.
To the faithful I am faithful;
to the unfaithful I am also faithful,
for Life is faithfulness.'
The Man of Calling lives very quietly in the world.
People look for him and listen out for him with surprise,
and the Man of Calling accepts them all as his children.

50

Going out is Life, going in is death.
Three out of ten are companions of Life.
Three out of ten are companions of death.
Three out of ten
are men who live
and thereby move towards the place of death.
What is the reason for this?
Because they want to create an increase of their lives.
I have heard that whosoever knows how to live life well
wanders through the land
and meets neither rhino nor tiger.
He walks through an army
and avoids neither armour nor weapons.
The rhino finds nothing to sink its horn into.
The tiger finds nothing to sink its claws into.
The weapon finds nothing to receive its sharpness.
Why is this so?
Because he has no mortal spot.

51

DAO generates.
Life nourishes.
Environment shapes.
Influences complete.

Therefore: all beings honour DAO
and cherish Life.
DAO is honoured,
Life is cherished,
without being outwardly appointed, just for themselves.

Therefore: DAO generates, Life nourishes,
makes grow, cares,
completes, keeps,
covers and protects.

52

The world has a beginning:
that is the Mother of the World.
Whosoever finds the mother
in order to know the sons;
whosoever knows the sons
and returns to the mother:
he will not be in danger all his life long.
Whosoever closes his mouth
and shuts his gates:
he will not be troubled all his life long.
Whosoever opens his mouth
and wants to set his affairs in order:
he cannot be helped all his life long.
To see the smallest means to be clear.
To guard wisdom means to be strong.
If one uses one's light
in order to return to this clarity
one does not endanger one's person.
This is called the hull of eternity.

53

If I really know what it means
to live in the great DAO,
then it is, above all, busy-ness
that I fear.
Where the great streets are beautiful and smooth
but the people prefer the sideroads;

where the rules of court are strict
but the fields are full of weeds;
where the barns are quite empty
but garments are beautiful and glamorous;
where everyone girds himself with a sharp sword;
where eating and drinking habits are refined
and goods are abundant:
there rules confusion, not government.

54

What is well planted will not be torn up.
What is well kept will not escape.
Whosoever leaves his memory to his sons and grandsons
will not fade away.
Whosoever moulds his person, his life becomes true.
Whosoever moulds his family, his life becomes complete.
Whosoever moulds his community, his life will grow.
Whosoever moulds his country, his life will become rich.
Whosoever moulds the world, his life will become broad.

Therefore: by your own person judge the person of the other.
By your own family judge the family of others.
By your community judge the community of others.
By your country judge the country of others.
By your world judge the world of others.
How do I know the nature of the world?
Just through this.

55

Whosoever holds fast to Life's completeness
is like a newborn infant:
Poisonous snakes do not bite it.
Scavenging animals do not lay hold of it.
Birds of prey do not hunt for it.
Its bones are weak, its sinews soft,
and yet it can grip firmly.
It does not yet know about man and woman,
and yet its blood stirs
because it has abundance of seed.

It can cry all day long
and yet its voice does not become hoarse
because it has abundance of peace.
To know peace means to be eternal.
To know eternity means to be clear.
To increase life is called happiness.
To apply one's strength to one's desire is called strong.
When things have grown strong they age.
For this is the counter-DAO,
and counter-DAO is close to the end.

56

He who knows does not speak.
He who speaks does not know.
One must close one's mouth
and shut one's gates,
blunt one's sharp wit,
dissolve one's confused thoughts,
moderate one's light,
make one's earthiness common.
This means hidden community with DAO.
Whosoever has this cannot be influenced by love,
nor can he be influenced by coldness.
He cannot be influenced by gain,
nor can he be influenced by loss.
He cannot be influenced by glory,
nor can he be influenced by lowliness.
Therefore is he the most glorious on earth.

57

To rule a state one needs the art of government;
for the craft of arms one needs
extraordinary talent.
But in order to win the world
one must be free of all busy-ness.
How do I know that this is the world's way?
The more things there are in the world that one must not do,
the more people are impoverished.
The more people have sharp implements,

the more house and state tumble into destruction.
The more people cultivate art and cleverness,
the more ominous signs arise.
The more law and order are propagated,
the more thieves and robbers there will be.

Therefore, the Man of Calling says:
If we do nothing
the people will change of themselves.
If we love stillness
the people right themselves of themselves.
If we undertake nothing
the people will become rich of themselves.
If we have no cravings
the people will become simple of themselves.

58

The ruler whose government is calm and unobtrusive,
his people are upright and honest.
The ruler whose government is sharp-witted and strict,
his people are underhand and unreliable.
Happiness rests on unhappiness;
unhappiness lies in wait for happiness.
But who is aware that the highest good is
not to have orders issued?
For otherwise order turns into oddities,
and good turns into superstition,
and the days of the people's delusion
are truly prolonged.

Thus also is the Man of Calling:
he sets an example without cutting others down to size;
he is conscientious without being hurtful;
he is genuine without being arbitrary;
he is bright without being blinding.

59

In leading Men and in the service of Heaven
there is nothing better than 'Limitation'.

For only through limitation
can one deal with things early on.
Through dealing with things early on
one redoubles the forces of Life.
Through these redoubled forces of Life
one rises to every occasion.
If we rise to every occasion,
no-one knows our limits.
If no-one knows our limits
we are capable of possessing the world.
If one possesses the Mother of the World
one gains eternal duration.
This is the DAO of the deep root,
of the firm ground,
of eternal existence
and of lasting sight.

60

A great country must be led
the way one fries small fish.
If one administers the world according to DAO,
then the ancestors do not swarm about as spirits.
Not that the ancestors are not spirits
but their spirits do not harm men.
Not only do the spirits not harm men,
the Man of Calling, too, does not harm them.
If then, these two powers do not harm one another,
then their Life-Forces are united in their effect.

61

By keeping itself downstream
a great realm becomes the unification of the world.
It is the female in the world.
The female always wins over the male by its stillness.
By its stillness it keeps below.
When the great realm puts itself below the small
it thereby wins the small realm over.
When the small realm puts itself below the great
it is thereby won over by the great realm.

Thus, by keeping below, the one wins over
and the other, by keeping below, is won over.
The great realm desires nothing
but to take part in the service of men.
Thus each attains what it wants:
but the great must remain below.

62

DAO is the homeland of all things,
the treasure of good men,
the protection of non-good men.
One may go to the market with beautiful words.
One may shine before others
with honourable conduct.
But the non-good among men – why should one throw them
    away?
Therefore the ruler has been appointed
and princes have their office.
Even if one had bejewelled sceptres
to send forth in a solemn quadriga:
nothing matches the gift
which is: offering this DAO
on one's knees to the ruler.
Why did the ancients so treasure this DAO?
Is it not because it has been said of it:
'Whosoever asks will receive;
Whosoever has sinned will be forgiven'?
Therefore is DAO the most exquisite thing on earth.

63

Whosoever practises non-action,
occupies himself with not being occupied,
finds taste in what does not taste:
he sees the great in the small and the much in the little.
He repays animosity with Life.
Plan what is difficult while it is still easy!
Do the great thing while it is still small!
Everything heavy on earth begins as something light.
Everything great on earth begins as something small.

Therefore: if the Man of Calling never does anything great,
then he can complete his great deeds.
Whosoever makes promises lightly,
surely he will not keep them.
He who takes many things lightly,
surely he will have much difficulty.
Therefore: if the Man of Calling gives consideration to
   difficulties
he shall never have difficulties.

64

What is still calm can easily be grasped.
What has not yet emerged can easily be considered.
What is still fragile can easily be broken.
What is still small can easily be scattered.
One must work on what is not yet there.
One must put in order what is not yet confused.
A tree trunk the size of a fathom
grows from a blade as thin as a hair.
A tower nine stories high
is built from a small heap of earth.
A journey of a thousand miles
starts in front of your feet.
Whosoever acts spoils it.
Whosoever keeps loses it.

Thus also is the Man of Calling:
He does not act, thus he spoils nothing.
He does not keep, thus he loses nothing.
People go after their affairs,
and always when they have nearly finished
they spoil it.
Pay attention to the end as much as to the beginning:
then nothing will be spoiled.

Thus also is the Man of Calling:
He desires desirelessness.
He does not desire goods that are hard to attain.
He learns non-learning.
He turns back to that which the multitude passes by.

Thereby he furthers the natural course of things
and does not dare to act.

65

Those of old who were competent
in ruling according to DAO
did not do it by enlightening the people
but by keeping the people unknowing.
The difficulty in leading the people
comes from their knowing too much.

Therefore: whosoever leads the state through knowledge
is the robber of the state.
Whosoever does not lead the state through knowledge
is the good fortune of the state.
Whosoever knows these two things has an ideal.
Always to know this ideal is hidden Life.
Hidden Life is deep, far-reaching,
different from all things,
but in the end it works the great success.

66

Rivers and seas are the kings of the streams
because they know how to keep themselves below.
Therefore are they the kings of the streams.

Thus also is the Man of Calling:
if he wants to stand above his people
he puts himself below them in speaking.
If he wants to be ahead of his people
he stands back.
Thus also:
He dwells in the high place
and the people are not burdened with him.
He stays in the prime place
and the people are not hurt by him.
Thus also:
the whole world is willing to advance him
and does not grow unwilling.

Because he does not quarrel
no-one in the world can quarrel with him.

67

All the world says that my DAO may be great
but, in a manner of speaking, useless.
Just because it is great,
therefore it is, in a manner of speaking, useless.
If it were useful
it would long ago have grown small.
I have three treasures
that I treasure and guard.
The first is called 'love';
the second is called 'sufficiency';
the third is called 'not daring to lead the world'.
Through love one may be courageous,
through sufficiency one may be generous.
If one does not dare to lead the world
one may be the head of complete men.
If one wants to be courageous without love,
if one wants to be generous without sufficiency,
if one wants to advance without standing back:
that means death.
If one has love in battle
one is victorious.
If one has it in defence
one is invincible.
Whom Heaven wants to save
him he protects through love.

68

Whosoever knows how to lead well
is not warlike.
Whosoever knows how to fight well
is not angry.
Whosoever knows how to conquer enemies
does not fight them.
Whosoever knows how to use men well
keeps himself below.

This is the Life that does not quarrel;
this is the power of using men;
this is the pole that reaches up to Heaven.

69

Among soldiers there is a saying:
I dare not play the lord and master,
I'd rather play the guest.
I dare not advance an inch,
I'd rather withdraw a foot.
This means walking without legs,
fighting without arms.

There is no greater misfortune
than underestimating the enemy.
If I underestimate the enemy
I am in danger of losing my treasure.
Where two armies confront each other in battle
the conqueror will be he who wins with a heavy heart.

70

My words are very easy to understand
and easy to carry out.
But no-one on earth can understand them
nor carry them out.
Words have an ancestor.
Deeds have a lord.
Because they are not understood
I am not understood.
It is precisely in being so rarely understood
that my value rests.
Therefore the Man of Calling
walks in haircloth
but in his bosom he guards a jewel.

71

To know non-knowledge
is the highest good.

Not to know what knowledge is
is a kind of suffering.
Only if one suffers from this suffering
does one become free of suffering.
If the Man of Calling does not suffer
it is because he suffers of this suffering:
therefore he does not suffer.

72

When people do not fear what is terrible,
then the great terror comes.
Do not make their dwellings narrow
nor their life vexed.
For it is because of this –
that they do not live in narrowness –
that their life does not become vexed.

Thus also is the Man of Calling:
He knows himself but does not want to shine.
He loves himself but does not seek honour for himself.
He removes the other and takes this.

73

Whosoever shows courage in daredevilry
will perish.
Whosoever shows courage without daredevilry
will stay alive.
Of these two the one brings gain,
the other harm.
However, who knows the reason
why Heaven hates one?

Thus also is the Man of Calling:
He sees the difficulties.
The DAO of Heaven does not quarrel
and yet has the gifts necessary to be victorious.
He does not speak
and yet he finds the right answer.
He does not beckon

and yet everything comes of itself.
He is tranquil
and yet is he competent in planning.
Heaven's nets are wide-meshed
but they lose nothing.

74

If the people do not fear death:
how can one frighten them with death?
But if I keep the people constantly
in fear of death and
if someone does strange things:
should I grab him and kill him?
Who dares do this?
There is always a power of death that kills.
To kill instead of leaving killing to this power of death
is as if one wanted to use the axe oneself
instead of leaving it to the carpenter.
Whosoever would use the axe
instead of leaving it to the carpenter
shall rarely get away
without injuring his hand.

75

When the people go hungry,
this comes from too much tax
being devoured by the high and mighty:
therefore the people go hungry.
When the people are hard to lead,
this comes from too much meddling
by the high and mighty:
therefore are they difficult to lead.
When the people take death too lightly,
this comes from life's abundance being sought too greedily
by the high and mighty:
therefore do they take death too lightly.
However, he who does not act for the sake of life,
he is better than the other to whom life is precious.

76

Man, when he enters life,
is soft and weak.
When he dies
he is hard and strong.
Plants, when they enter life,
are soft and tender.
When they die
they are dry and stiff.
Therefore: the hard and the strong
are companions of death;
the soft and the weak
are companions of life.

Therefore: when weapons are strong they are not victorious.
When trees are strong they are cut down.
The strong, the great, is below.
The soft, the weak, is above.

77

The DAO of Heaven: how it resembles the archer!
He presses down what is high
and raises that which is low.
Whatever has too much he reduces,
whatever does not have enough he completes.
It is the DAO of Heaven
to reduce what has too much
and to complete what does not have enough.
Man's DAO is not so.
He reduces what does not have enough,
in order to offer it to what has too much.
But who is capable of offering to the world
that of which he has too much?
Only he who has DAO.

Thus also is the Man of Calling:
he works and does not keep.
When the work is done he does not tarry with it.
He does not desire to show off his importance to others.

78

In the whole world there is nothing softer
and weaker than water.
And yet nothing measures up to it
in the way it works upon that which is hard.
Nothing can change it.
Everyone on earth knows
that the weak conquers the strong
and the soft conquers the hard –
but no-one is capable of acting accordingly.

Thus also spoke the Man of Calling:
'Whosoever takes upon himself the filth of the realm,
he is the lord at the earth's sacrifices.
Whosoever takes upon himself the misfortune of the realm,
he is the king of the world.'
True words are as if contrary.

79

If one placates great anger
and yet there remains anger:
how could this be good?
Therefore the Man of Calling adheres to his duty
and demands nothing of others.

Therefore: whosoever has Life
adheres to his duty;
whosoever does not have Life
adheres to his right.

80

A country shall be small
and its populace small in number.
Implements that multiply men's strength
shall not be used.
People are to take death seriously
and shall not travel far away.
Even though there be ships and carriages

no-one shall travel in them.
Even though there be armour and weapons
no-one shall employ them.
Let the people tie knots in ropes
and use them instead of script.
Make their food sweet
and their garments beautiful,
their dwellings peaceful
and their customs joyful.
Neighbouring countries may be within eyesight
so that one can hear the cocks crow and the dogs bark
on either side.
And yet shall people die at great age
without having travelled hither and thither.

81

True words are not beautiful,
beautiful words are not true.
Competence does not persuade,
persuasion is not competent.
The sage is not learned,
the learned man is not wise.
The Man of Calling does not heap up possessions.
The more he does for others,
the more he possesses.
The more he gives to others,
the more he has.
The DAO of Heaven is 'furthering without causing harm'
The DAO of the Man of Calling is to be effective without
    quarrelling.

COMMENTARY:
The Teaching of Lao Zi

1 DAO

Ancient Chinese theism taught that there was a god in Heaven on whom the world depended absolutely, and who rewarded good men and punished the evil. This god has human consciousness. He allowed the elect saints, like King Wen, to be his entourage. He was capable of getting angry and meting out punishment if men were evil; but ultimately he would always forgive them and have mercy on them, if their priest and representative, the son of Heaven, purified himself in the right way and approached him with sacrificial offerings. The Earth as mother was partner to this father in Heaven. There was also – though they did not impinge on the monotheistic foundation – an abundance of natural and ancestral spirits who were dependent on Heaven, but nevertheless had their own specific tasks, rather like public officials under a king.

This religious viewpoint had been wrecked under the impact of terrible and extreme events when no god in Heaven showed his face to intervene on behalf of poor, tortured, yet innocent men. It is with Lao Zi that the radical elimination of religious anthropomorphism begins. In his view, Heaven and Earth have no human feelings of love: to them all beings are like straw dogs. These straw dogs are placed in a shrine and clothed in beautifully embroidered garments in preparation for sacrificial festivities. The priest of the dead fasts and purifies himself in preparation for their sacrifice. However, once they have served their purpose, they are thrown away so that passers-by tread on their heads and backs, and the gatherers of firewood pick them up and burn them. It is the same with the relationship between Nature and all living beings. During their allotted time they readily find the table of life laid for them, and everything prepared for their use. But their moment passes and they are discarded and trampled upon, and the stream of life passes them by.

However, Lao Zi is far from considering the course of Nature to be accidental or unruly. He is free of all scepticism and pessimism. He does not simply fight against popular religion, but replaces it with something that is of a higher order, and leads further. From the ancient wisdom of the *Book of Changes* (*Yi Jing*), he had concluded that the essence of the world is not a static or mechanical condition. The world undergoes continuous change and transformation. All that exists is, just because it exists, subject to death: for although birth and death are opposites, they are nevertheless inextricably linked to each other. Yet, although everything that exists passes away, there is no reason to say 'All is vanity', for the same *Book of Changes* also shows that all transformations take place according to fixed laws. The *Book of Changes* expresses the view that the whole phenomenal world rests upon a polar opposition of forces: creative and receptive, One and Two, light and shadow, positive and negative, male and female – are all examples of the polar forces that bring about change and transformation. One must imagine these forces as primary principles which are at rest. The world view of the *Book of Changes* is not one of simple cosmic dualism.

Instead it understands the forces it speaks about as being themselves in a process of continuous change. The One splits itself and becomes Two; the Two unite and become One. The creative and the receptive unite and generate the world. Therefore Lao Zi says that the One engenders the Two, the Two engenders the Three, the Three engenders all things. This is represented in the *Book of Changes* by the coming together of the undivided line of the creative, and the divided line of the receptive in the formation of eight three-levelled primary trigrams; the combination of these represent the whole world of possible constellations of 'time'.

But Lao Zi had also concluded from the *Book of Changes* that this all-embracing change in the phenomenal world is not a matter of blind coincidence or chance. The *Book of Changes* speaks of three kinds of transformation:

1. Cyclical change, such as the change of the seasons. One state of things changes into another, but in the course of such changes the original state of things is restored. So, for example,

winter is followed by spring, summer and autumn, but autumn in turn is followed by winter, and thus the cycle of transformations is completed. Cosmic events are like the rising and setting of the sun in the course of the day and the year: the waxing and waning of the moon, and the spring and autumn equinoxes, are examples of such transformations.

2. The second kind of transformation is represented by progressive development. One state of things progressively changes into another, but the line does not revert to its original condition. Progress and development continue with time. Such are the days of men: one is not equal to another – although they are also included in the great cycle of the seasons – but each one contains the sum total of the experiences of the preceding days plus the new day's experiences.

3. Finally, the third kind is the immutable law that works through all these transformations. This law causes all movements to become visible in a definite manner. If one observes the phenomena in Heaven and Earth they appear overwhelming in scale and impact, and confusing in their manifoldness and multiplicity. According to this law, the principle of the creative is the active force which works through time. When this force first enters into action it does so lightly and hardly noticeably, so that the effects can be quite easily traced. Objects of great force or density develop only gradually out of the light and the minimal.

The receptive principle is the principle of spatial mobility. When this reacts to the stimulus of the creative, all spatial change is at first quite simple and gradual, and easily recognisable without confusion. It is only in the further course of events that this simple and gradual change accelerates into a confusing multitude of impressions. And so it is important to recognise the seeds or sources of growth in all things. This is the point from which one has to start if one wants to see clearly and work effectively, just as all effects in Nature develop from the easy and simple to the difficult and multiple. For all these laws work not as a result of an external necessity, but out of an immanent organic vitality, in the freedom of entelechy's own law.

In the final analysis it is the great polarity *tai ji*, the unity beyond all duality, beyond all occurrence, even beyond all existence, that lies at the root of all these changes. The changes proceed in a firm and meaningful way, the Way of Heaven (*tian dao*), whose equivalent on earth is the Way of Man (*ren dao*). For it is one of the most important principles of the *Book of Changes* that there is a general relationship and harmony between macrocosm and microcosm, between the images sent from Heaven and the social and cultural thoughts formed by the saints and rulers in imitation of these images. In the *Book of Changes* we find the astronomical/astrological foundations of Chinese religion shining through in the concepts of the Way of Heaven and the Way of Man. These ideas are taken further in the philosophy of Confucius; but Lao Zi also built his philosophy upon them. For Lao Zi did have a philosophy, even if he only left us a few aphorisms: these aphorisms contain an organic body of thought, which will reveal itself to anyone capable of grasping its true context.

Lao Zi begins by searching for a fundamental principle for his view of the world. Confucianism had come to rest at the image of Heaven. Heaven was somehow thought of as a personal being. It was conceived as something higher and purer than the god of popular religon, Shang Di, which had shown strongly anthropomorphic features. But at moments of high inner tension, Confucius would always speak in such a way that one had a clear sense of his religious relationship to a Heaven which 'knew' him, which entrusted the traditions of civilisation to him, and to which one could pray at times of inner crisis. For Lao Zi this was still not the highest and the ultimate. For him, the highest and the ultimate was beyond personality, even beyond any observable and definable existence. It was not a 'something' beside or above other 'things'. But it was not nothingness either; instead, it was something that eludes all human forms of thinking.

For 'this' there is, of course, no name. For all names stem from experience, whereas it is 'this' that makes all experience possible. It was only in order to speak about it, and for want of a better expression, that he finally called it DAO, to resolve his predicament; and he called it 'great'.

In doing so he took over and transformed an existing expression. The DAO of Heaven and the DAO of Man had been known since ancient times, but absolute DAO had not. DAO means 'way'. But, given the manner in which Lao Zi uses the term, one cannot translate it as 'way' or 'faith'. In the Chinese language there are two words for 'way'. One of them is *lu*. It is written as a combination of the symbols for 'foot' and 'every'. It is what every foot treads: the way that comes about by being trodden. This term might be used figuratively, for the modern concept of 'law of Nature', for this is also conceived as existing because events tend to occur in accordance with it. The other word for 'way' is DAO. It is written as a combination of the symbols for 'head' and 'to go'. This gives us a meaning quite different from that of the word *lu*. It means 'the way that leads to a set goal', 'the direction', 'the prescribed way'. It also means 'to talk' and 'to lead'. It seems that the symbol was first used to indicate the astronomic course of the stars. Since ancient times the equator was called 'the red way', and the apparent path of the sun among the stars in the course of the year, the 'yellow way'. These ways are not random or accidental: they have meaning, significance. And it is in this sense that Lao Zi uses the word. DAO is neither something material nor something spiritual, but all meaning emanates from it. It is that which is ultimately free. It provides its own direction while everything else receives its meaning from something outside itself: man receives it from the Earth, the Earth from Heaven, and Heaven from DAO.

When Lao Zi speaks of DAO, he is careful to remove everything that could point to existence of any kind. He is working, then, at a level totally different from anything that belongs to the phenomenal world. DAO is earlier than Heaven and Earth. One cannot tell where it comes from: it is even earlier than God. It rests upon itself, and is immutable, rapt in eternal, cyclical movement. It is the beginning of Heaven and Earth, in other words, of temporal and spatial existence. It is the mother of all created beings. In another place he also calls it 'the ancestor of all beings'.

Lao Zi quotes an ancient adage in which DAO is compared to the spirit of the empty valley, to the mysterious female, flowing uninterrupted like a waterfall as though it were eternal, its mysterious entrance the root of Heaven and Earth. This concept is probably based on an ancient magic formula for the invocation of the spirit of the pictogram *Kan* ☵ . It represents the moon, and also the heavenly water that flows between steep embankments. It is the darkly mysterious, the dangerous, 'the Abysmal', the highest, freely-moving wisdom, the inexhaustible.

It was originally thought of as female, and it is only since the end of the second millennium BC that it has been called male. It stands in the north or in the west, always in the dark half of the cycle of the sun. Its symbol in the starry sky is the dark warrior, a mysterious union of serpent and tortoise. In ancient times it was no doubt connected with black magic. (According to Lie Zi, this formula is derived from the writings of Huang Di. It is quite possible that Lao Zi also took it from another source, just as so many passages in the *Dao De Jing* are quotations.) In this formula Lao Zi found features which agreed with what he understood as DAO, and so he used it as a parable. He likens DAO to water on other occasions as well, because it is powerful through 'keeping below', and flowing in places which are generally despised; or he finds likenesses of DAO in the valley, the sea, or the deep rivers, because they all 'keep themselves below', and are able to receive all the water that flows into them without ever filling up or overflowing. For DAO is empty and never becomes full.

Although it is said to have no existence, DAO is not simply 'nothingness'. For from nothingness nothing can come. DAO is neither temporal nor spatial. When one looks for it one cannot see it; when one listens for it one cannot hear it; when one tries to touch it one cannot feel it. Yet this non-spatiality and non-temporality somehow contains the makings of manifoldness: forms and images, but without form, without content. One cannot discern front or back in DAO. It often seems as though it were there, but then it recedes again into non-existence. DAO is therefore on a level beyond existence. It is nothing 'real', for then it would be a 'thing' amongst other 'things'. But on the other hand it is not so unreal that real things cannot proceed from it.

It follows that nothing can be positively asserted about DAO. Every positive assertion about it is wrong, because it is beyond what can be affirmed or denied. For this reason Lao Zi always strives to set limits to his assertions. He speaks in parables. He says 'it seems', 'it may be called', 'it is as if', 'it is about like' . . . – in other words he always uses indefinite, allusive terms. For DAO can be neither perceived nor known. All assertions about it are only pointers towards an immediate experience that cannot be expressed in words.

For the same reason, the term DAO is not a concept. The

living experience which is expressed by the term lies beyond our conceptual powers because it is immediate, direct. Nor is it a subject for study. Whoever knows it does not speak about it, and whoever does speak about it does not know it. The more one tries to describe and define it, the further one gets from it. Therefore the road to DAO is opposite to the road to learning. Learning involves increasing one's experiences, and always accumulating more. If one turns towards DAO, however, one decreases the amount of conscious experiences at one's disposal until one arrives at non-action. If one practises non-action, nothing remains not done. Everything then comes about of its own accord.

In all this Lao Zi is fully aware that his DAO is not a scientific achievement. When the highest kind of men hear about it, they act in accordance. Lesser men doubt: now they hold on to it, now it escapes them again. When ordinary men hear about it, they laugh loudly. If they do not laugh it is not the true DAO.

In order to understand what Lao Zi meant by DAO we must now go back to mystical experiences. A similar concept can be found in Mahayana Buddhism. Through concentration and meditation one reaches the state of *Samādhi*, in which the psyche reaches beyond consciousness into the sphere of superconsciousness. If these experiences are genuine, they do indeed lead into the depths of being which lie beyond the entire phenomenal world. The visible form of such events is known from certain parapsychological phenomena, and has become the object of scientific research. The experience of DAO, however, can never become an object of scientific research. What we are dealing with here is a primal phenomenon in the highest sense of this term: one can only marvel in awe, but one cannot trace its origins or fathom it out. The experience of DAO is like all immediate experience. For instance, when I perceive the colour 'yellow', or 'blue', the physical processes that take place in the eye can be investigated even though there is much room for speculation; but this does not amount to a real grasp of the perception itself. And one can never succeed in conveying the experience to anyone who has not had it. Whoever has had such an experience – to him Lao Zi's words are immediately understandable, and capable of helping him on his way.

Lao Zi attributes not only psychological, but also cosmic significance to DAO. In this he is correct for the 'cosmos' is not something that exists objectively, quite independent of experience. Every organism exists in a setting or context, and the kind of context is related to the organism's particular skills and capacities. By presenting his DAO in such a way that it is neither temporally nor spatially determined, Lao Zi offers the conditions for every experience and for the whole universe. All experience depends upon interpretation, on adducing meaning. DAO is that meaning which confers significance upon all that is, and in this way calls all that is into existence. DAO creates all that is created, but because it even creates the creative, it has itself never entered the phenomenal world.

However, Lao Zi does not make scientifically verifiable statements about DAO. Given the nature of the issue, he cannot offer proof but he points to ways in which one may come to the experience of DAO. We shall talk about these ways later on. At this point it is important to proceed from the metapsychic and metaphysical world to the phenomenal world.

2 THE PHENOMENAL WORLD

DAO, or essence, is unfolded in reality, that is in the phenomenal world. This world can be the subject of scientific research, for in it are things which can be named and from which concepts can be formed. However, the world of reality is not something different from DAO. Lao Zi is hardly proposing a theory about an earthly world emanating from a higher world. The world of DAO is not an abstract entity but, as we have seen, manifoldness is immanent in it. In DAO there are images, seeds, things. It is true that these images are not distinct and separate phenomena: they are potentially present within the unitary DAO. But these images and things are the germinal potencies of reality; they condition all the phenomena that are found in our world.

In order to understand what Lao Zi means by these 'images' one can refer to Plato's theory of ideas. Unlike Plato, however, Lao Zi did not develop his theory of ideas dialectically. One cannot gain an understanding of his thought by a process of abstraction; instead, a primal view from one's inner depths will produce these images for oneself. These images or forms are non-corporeal, non-spatial. They are like fleeting images passing over the smooth surface of a mirror. These 'images of things' are the seeds of reality. Just as the acorn contains the oak, ungraspable, invisible and yet completely distinct as an entelechy, so the 'things' of reality are contained in these seed-images. Certain seeds come to the fore and develop in a clear and definite way, because these seeds are totally genuine. The reliability of occurrence is founded in them. One kind of seed will never bring forth a 'thing' of another kind. But even when they do come to the fore in this way, they never become solidified into existence. They return to the realm of the non-real, leaving behind the dead and empty husks of phenomenality to which they had once given a soul. Life itself has not died – even after the 'straw dogs' of phenomenal existence have been discarded and trampled underfoot.

As I see it, Lao Zi's teaching on ideas is a further development of the teaching on seeds in the *Book of Changes*. What is there called 'seed' – that from which a successive line of events develops in accordance with the fixed law of changes – becomes Lao Zi's 'image', which as an invisible, immanent law directs the becoming and the passing away of the 'things' of reality. Occasionally Lao Zi puts forward a curious deduction of his own from the *Book of Changes*, as when he says that the one creates the Two, the Two creates the Three and the Three creates all things. In this way he sets forth and develops the complementarity of opposites: wherever the One – as decision, as limit, or line, or in some other way – is posited, all that is other, i.e. not One, is simultaneously given. By the coming forth of the One the Two is created; by the Two joining the One the Three comes about. These three then form a different and greater entity which already contains the manifold. Beyond this process one cannot go without confronting multiplicity. And therefore it is said that the Three creates all things.

In order to understand this philosophical approach one can refer to Neoplatonism in ancient philosophy. Early Christian meditations on the Trinity, in which progression to the Four produces Lucifer, are also closely related to this thinking. Similar ideas can even be found in more recent philosophy: Hegel's dialectic, with its thesis, antithesis and synthesis, where synthesis then becomes the thesis for the next series, the departure point for all that follows – is based on an approach very much like Lao Zi's.

The two primal powers from which the visible world as the Third is born, are Heaven and Earth, *yang* (the light power) and

73

yin (the dark power), the positive and the negative line, the temporal and the spatial – in other words the opposites from which the phenomenal world proceeds. Heaven and Earth are compared to a musician and a flute. The flute is empty, but the breath of the flute-player brings forth sounds from it; and the more it is played, the more manifold are the sounds. Endless melodies come forth in uninterrupted succession, but they are bewitched by the instrument which is not, in itself, the sound. The flute is the Earth, the breath is Heaven. But who sets the breath in motion? Who is the great flute-player who lures a colourful world out of this magic flute? In the final analysis it is DAO. It has no exterior cause: it moves in free naturalness, out of its innermost essence.

Thus DAO occupies a dual position in the phenomenal world. It releases the seed of ideas into existence where they unfold into things that extend in space and time. It is also the great flute-player with his magic flute. It is the ancestor of all created beings, the root of Heaven and Earth, the mother of all things. Thus it turns one side towards existence. Nevertheless it is impossible to grasp it, to look at it, or overhear it. It returns into non-existence where it is unreachable and eternal, because all things under Heaven evolve from what exists. But existence itself evolves from the non-existent, and returns to non-existence in which it is forever rooted. This 'non-existent' DAO is the driving force within all that moves in the phenomenal world. The functioning, the effectiveness of all that is 'existence' rests on 'non-existence'. Reality is, in a way, loosened up by gaps and absences or empty spaces; thus it becomes usable and useful by their being 'nothing', that is empty, just as vessels or chambers become usable and useful because they contain 'nothing', by their hollow, empty space. Thus is DAO effective in the phenomenal world: by non-action.

Having shown how the phenomenal world proceeds from DAO, through the intermediary of ideas, we must now consider Lao Zi's theory of cognition, his teaching on concepts. The problem of the relationship between 'name' and 'reality' plays an important part in the Chinese philosophy of his time. Although later rationalists have increasingly adopted a nominalism which considers a 'name' as something completely arbitrary that never reaches 'reality', the classical philosophies of Confucius and Lao Zi are unanimous in considering concepts or names, as somehow corresponding to reality, or as capable of being made to concur with reality, so that they become a medium for establishing order in reality. For Confucius the 'rectification of concepts' is the most important means of establishing order in human relations and in society: empirical relationships must be made to concur with rational relationships, so that order will prevail in society. In the family for instance, the man who is called 'father' must be as a father in order to answer to the rational concept of 'father'; in the same way the son must be as a son, and the other members of the family accordingly; only then will the family have its proper order. A similar principle applies to all other fields of life. This line of thought is also derived from the *Book of Changes*: there we find the concept that Heaven reveals the primal images which the leaders and prophets of calling take as guidelines for their cultural institutions. The trigrams and hexagrams in the *Book of Changes* depict all possible world situations, and from the laws which govern their changes one can draw conclusions about the changes that occur at a cosmic level.

Lao Zi also puts forward a theory of concepts. The 'images' which are immanent in DAO can somehow be given names, but these names are secret and unutterable. Just as DAO cannot be expressed, so these cannot be expressed. There are, of course, names that can be named, but these are not the highest, not eternal. If, however, the names that can be named are correctly chosen, they somehow come close to existence – even if only as 'guests of reality', not as reality's masters. They can serve in some way to create order, to pass on tradition and thus preserve the continuity of human activity.

In this manner, the world of essence may be named 'non-existence', and the phenomenal world called 'existence'. In that case, 'non-existence' is the beginning of Heaven and Earth, and 'existence' is the mother of all beings. If one concentrates on non-existence one will see the secrets of essence; if one concentrates on existence one will see the external, three-dimensional appearance of things. But one must not think that this implies a dual world, a present world and a world beyond. The difference between the two states exists only in name: the name of the one is existence, and of the other non-existence. Yet although the names are different, they both represent the same fact: the dark secret, out of whose depths all miracles flow.

Once one has names that can be articulated, one has the instruments for cognition. These concepts, given as names to things, provide one with a means of fastening on to things; and one can then use the name instead of the thing for thinking, just as one uses letters instead of numbers in algebra. Using concepts, one can express laws as formulae, and numbers conform to them. As long as reality, 'things', are used as checks and balances, names and concepts are usable and useful. They can then be used to define the products of cognition. All such definitions, of course, have a necessarily divisive quality. If all men recognise the beautiful as beautiful, then thereby the ugly is already posited. Knowledge is gained by a process of comparison and definition, and is therefore necessarily bound up with the phenomenal world, which is divided into pairs of opposites.

This line of thought leads us even further afield. Having these concepts as tools for the cognition of reality, Man can, in the end, use them quite independently – that is, independent of reality. He can produce concepts which do not correspond to any primal image in reality. He can isolate things from their existential context, and establish something that does not exist as the goal and object which he strives for. In this way 'names' become the creators of desire. By using them in this way he can secure not only what he already has, but also what he does not have. For Lao Zi this is the instance of original sin in cognition. Reality may only be the appearance and the exterior of DAO, but it is nevertheless somehow related to it. Here, however, one is confronted with a teleological, purpose-built world, in which goals and purposes are not real but the creations of human desire, to be attained through human effort. This engenders a craving for what is not one's own but belongs to someone else. Since the owner of this property will not readily let it go, strife and battle will follow and the result will be theft and murder; and this is the opposite of DAO.

In this way, the phenomenal world becomes a world of evil for Lao Zi, a world of craven desires, bound up with the presence of 'names'. Men enter into a maze of error because of it. Perceptions are no longer pure representations in which the will has no voice. They blind and seduce men, and the delusion of desire sends them mad. Reason is at work and the actual quantity of knowledge appears to increase. But the more acutely reason works the more acute reason becomes, the more mankind moves away from DAO. Therefore Lao Zi holds that culture and knowledge should not be fostered any further, but harmlessly assimilated into the context of nature instead. Faced with the excessive development of rationality one must return to the nameless (non-conceptual) simplicity, to the condition in which one lets DAO take its harmless course, without attaching names to it. In this way the connection between the great mother and her child, man, will be re-established.

3 ON THE ATTAINMENT OF DAO

Lao Zi is far from merely offering a theory for understanding the world. He wants to point a way out of the confusion of the phenomenal world, and into the eternal. To find this way, and to walk upon it, is to attain DAO. A dual path leads to this attainment: one goes by way of existence and the other by non-existence. If one wants to find DAO in existence, one should look at phenomena in such a way that one avoids becoming entangled in its web. For these are only the external forms of DAO. Everything in the phenomenal world is somehow an effect of DAO: the high and the low, the beautiful and the ugly, good and evil. Nothing exists that does not have its existence through DAO. It does not refuse itself even to the merest grain of dust. But one searches in vain for DAO in reality if one has goals and designs, or schemes. The more one searches the world with definite goals and designs in mind the more one fosters wants and desires, and the more one becomes tied up in isolation. In this way one reaches counter-DAO; and that soon comes to an end. The specific direction one takes makes no difference at all. Whether one seeks pleasure, colour, sounds, delicacies, exciting games, or rare goods: all will have the effect of entangling one more and more deeply in the web of delusion. Similarly, it is an illusion to aim at saintliness and wisdom, love and duty, skill and gain, learning and knowledge. For in doing so one exaggerates one pole only, and this necessarily has the effect of evoking its opposite.

For DAO is like an archer. It complements every extreme by its opposite. What is high is brought low, what is low is raised up. It is the DAO of Heaven to reduce what is plentiful, and increase what is lacking.

Therefore the way from existence to DAO leads through an

acknowledgment of the opposites in the phenomenal world. The more one is free from the delusions of desire, the more free one becomes of one's own ego. No longer will one view the world scourged by hopes and fears; instead it will be seen merely as an object of contemplation. Enormous powers rage like cloudbursts and cyclones. But a cyclone does not last a morning before it is over. One realises how strong weapons are, and yet they remain without victory; how strong a tree can be, and yet it is cut down. Happiness depends upon sorrow. Sorrow lies in wait for happiness. By recognising this one will succeed in eliminating the ego. For it is this tiny ego, mistaking the space between birth and death for life, that is the true source of all delusion. Desiring possessions and achievements for this brief span of time, realising these desires with the magic of a 'name' – which both causes the object of desire to be known, and is the cause of that desire – this is the source of the delusions that obscure and conceal DAO. Thus even grace is something disquieting, and honour a great torment. The persona/ego is perpetually restless, whether it receives grace or loses it, and it is the same with honour. If one eliminates the persona there will no longer be evil of any kind. Yet DAO is effective in sovereign certainty, even when the ego is darkened by desires: in fact, even these desires are an effect of DAO in accordance with fixed laws. Nothing can be other than it is. The only task is not to block one's way. Thus one's view of the world will become free of delusion, and pure; one will look at life's game with an inner calm. Then one will know that living and dying only means 'going out' and 'going in'. If one follows the eternal law and is not beholden anywhere, never becomes hardened or rigid, one will remain within the flow of DAO, and the forces of death, which bear down only when something hardens or solidifies will no longer have any power.

And so the external way, via existence, is one way towards DAO, which is, after all, unfolded in all existence – provided one is free of delusion, and looks in pure contemplation upon the skilful work of the mother, who spins her threads and lets them flow like the streams of a waterfall, continuous, incessant. But one knows that this veil is alive, that it is in constant movement, knowing no hesitation, no desire, no ego, no duration: πάντα ῥεῖ panta rei: everything is in a state of flux.

This pure contemplation which sees the eternal DAO in what is transitory, is only one of the two paths. The other path leads through non-existence. It leads man to the sight of the secret forces, to a union with the mother. What had previously been only a spectacle now becomes living experience. One arrives at the One-without-a-Two, the dark source from which Heaven and Earth, all beings and all forces spring. It is there that insights which one cannot talk about, which one must worship in silence, are briefly and brilliantly illuminated. The way of silence leads away from everything personal. For what is personal is only a mortal husk which one moves along as one walks through life. This path leads into stillness, where everything visible dissolves into insubstantial *maya*. It leads back from multiplicity into unity. But one has to prepare oneself inwardly for this way. One must work on one's own soul so that it can hold on to the One without breaking apart. For this is the criterion: when a sage of the highest kind hears about DAO he adheres to it; when a sage of a lower kind hears about DAO he wavers: now he has it, now he loses it again. But one must get beyond this wavering if one wants to gain entry to the innermost sanctum. The first step is to achieve complete unity. Then comes the task of making all the forces of the soul supple. No rigidity must be allowed to remain – the kind that produces a condition of spurious unity – for one's living experience must be utterly simple and easy. The inner forces must begin to flow, must overcome all hindrances. One must become like an infant that can sustain all effort without tiring just because it is soft and supple, not rigid. This inner liquescence does not, however, mean dispersion: it is the precondition of a lasting inner composure. It is a state of relaxation and equilibrium that can no longer be disturbed because it has become certain. Only now does the contemplation of the depths of essence become possible, for now the soul-mirror becomes pure, free of stain and pliable. It no longer wants to hold on to any impression, but follows the stimuli that arise from the depths, without any will of its own. Now it experiences the opening and closing of the gates of Heaven. It sees the invisible, feels the ungraspable. It is beyond existence, far below, where the mothers dwell. It witnesses the mysterious processes of life, and keeps itself still and forbearing like a mother-bird brooding over the secret of growing life in the egg. And the egg-shell breaks. Unification with the ultimate DAO takes place. The son has found the mother . . . Now clarity permeates everything, the great, redeeming recognition of the One-without-a-Two.

As a result of this recognition one no longer wants to separate and define the opposites in the phenomenal world, but accepts them and unites them in higher synthesis. One recognises the male-creative principle in oneself, and yet holds fast to the female-receptive; one recognises honour, and yet stays willingly in shame. Therefore one remains free of all the demands and desires of the persona and returns to original simplicity. Whoever recognises his child-like nature and guards and protects DAO, the great mother of the world, will not be in danger all his life. Whoever keeps the gates shut and his mouth closed will not know drudgery all his life. He sees the small, he guards the yielding, and in this way his persona is spared all harm. Whoever knows how to safeguard his life is not afraid of the tiger or rhinoceros, and is even capable of walking right through a crowd of armed men without armour or weapons; for since nothing in him evokes resistance he has no mortal point in which he can be wounded.

The man who has attained DAO will base all of his actions on this knowledge. He will always work on that which does not yet exist, and set to order what is not yet in a state of confusion. For the seeds of all things already exist in the invisible, as the *Book of Changes* relates. It is important to work upon these seeds, so that whatever is put into them will unfold as the seed grows all by itself, without any further action or external interference. This organic influence upon the seeds of future events is the decisive effect of the man who has attained DAO. Whatever has been planted in this manner will never be uprooted. A good wanderer leaves no trace behind him; a good gatekeeper needs no lock or bolt. Whoever knows how to work upon these seeds also reveals his secret power in letting the opposing forces have their way at first. Whatever one wants to compress one must first allow to expand fully. Only when a power has almost exhausted itself through its own efforts can another power overcome it with ease.

These secret laws do, of course contain formulae that can lead to black magic, and they have in fact been exploited by the magical forms of Daoism, just as they were exploited by the Japanese method of *ju-jitsu*, or by the state Daoism of Han Fei Zi. But while Lao Zi sees the mechanisms of magical activity, he is not interested in applying this knowledge in a narrow or one-sided way. His greatness consists in penetrating to the final unity of the cosmos, whose silent calmness no longer contains opposites that can be exploited for one purpose or another. Here we see the difference between his way and the way of knowledge. Knowledge goes further and further out into the world, seeks and searches, and piles up more and more facts. But in order to attain DAO one must penetrate deeper and deeper into the 'within', until one reaches the point of unity where the individual personality is in touch with cosmic totality. From this point of unity a view of the great essence becomes possible. Without going out of doors one can perceive the world. Without looking out of the window one can see the DAO of Heaven. Whoever has this standpoint does not wander about, and yet he reaches his goal. He looks for nothing and yet is he clear about all things. He does not act and yet he brings about completion. He will lead his life as a personality but the persona, the mask which is the ego, will no longer deceive him. He will play his part like everybody else but will keep himself away from the hustle and bustle of others. For he has become free of delusion, and values nourishment from the great mother alone.

4 WORLDLY WISDOM

This would be the place to talk about Lao Zi's ethics. But ethics in the sense of rational laws, and legislation for correct action are not to be found in the *Dao De Jing*. On the contrary, Lao Zi turns against morality and against preached moral virtues, just as he turns against culture (or 'civilisation') and the values it cherishes. In his view, morality and culture are closely related to one another. Every culture is based on a certain morality. Like culture, morality deviates from the maternal grounds of the natural, and for this he condemns them. This condemnation is aphoristic, often expressed in paradoxical phrases – rather like Nietzsche's attacks on morals – and this means it is not easy to follow a consistent line in Lao Zi's position. For he is a Proteus who eludes our crude grasp by continuous transformation. He gives us few words that can be understood in a literal sense, as expressing his cut and dried convictions. Lao Zi did not write for philistines, and it even seems as though he secretly enjoyed it when philistines laughed at him.

By tracing the reasons which led him to condemn what was in his own time, aimed as 'morality', at directing the actions of men, we will find the ways which Lao Zi points out for men's correct action opening up before us. He traces ethics back from duty to Nature, from man to DAO, from the artificial to the self-evident and simple. The first reason he condemns morality is on account of the formal principle that morality commands and gives orders. It uses the words 'Thou shalt'. It needs laws and yardsticks. But with laws and yardsticks one achieves the opposite of what one wants. The more the laws glitter, and the more the cumbersome 'Thou shalt' is spread about, the more thieves and robbers there will be; for it is a law of human nature to resist all coercion. And so morality is the most paltry and superficial of all motivations held up to men. Morals fight with a blunt sword and achieve the opposite of what is really wanted. Waving one's arms about and resorting to force does not sustain morality either. Morality lacks the grace of self-evidence. Thus one finds that morality flourishes especially in times of decline. When men are no longer naturally kind to one another, morality blossoms. When kinfolk are disunited, filial duty and love will be the supreme virtues. When disorder and confusion reign in the state there will be faithful servants. For only then do these things become special; before this they are not even mentioned. In this way morality always requires the foil of its opposite in order to shine. Its brightness only reveals itself in exceptional circumstances; and just because of this it also condemns itself.

However, it is not only the formal principle of the 'Thou shalt', of the law, which Lao Zi turns against. He also attacks the principal content of morality, the ideal of the 'good' and the 'virtues'. The good is not something absolute: it is always part of a mutually complementing pair of opposites. Just as there is no light without shadow so there is no good without evil. If all men affirm the good as good, then evil is thereby already posited. The opposition between good and evil is no more crucial than the one between the friendly affirmation 'certainly' and the hesitant affirmation 'probably'. Lao Zi resolutely takes his standpoint beyond good and evil. The absolute is beyond such worldly opposites; it is where opposites are joined to produce a higher unity.

What is more, there is no universal agreement about what is good and what is evil. These are different things at different times and in different places. Here we may remind ourselves of the reported conversations between Lao Zi and Confucius, for the remarks attributed to Lao Zi in that context are quite in line with his expositions in the *Dao De Jing*. In these discussions he speaks of morality and customs as simply relics from times past, and says that the spirit of the ages is something unique which transforms itself continually, and which disappears irretrievably once the rulers who created those customs are dead and gone. The customs and laws of the rulers of antiquity were not great because they were congruent with one another, but because they brought about order – just as different fruits may taste quite different, and yet all taste good. Customs and laws must both be adapted to the particular times, and continually changed. Morality is therefore something that is conditioned, not something absolute.

The greatest fault of all morals is that they make man too conscious and too goal-orientated. They are therefore something that takes away his capacity for harmlessness and simplicity. Lao Zi expects a whole range of ill effects to result from this. Whoever cherishes Life does not act and has no designs or schemes. Whoever cherishes love acts but has no designs. Whoever cherishes justice acts and has designs. Whoever cherishes morals acts and if he receives no response waves his arms about and resorts to force, in order to subject men to a system of morals. And so morals are paltry versions of faith and trust and the source of confusion, and designs are the sham of DAO and the beginning of folly. Morals – and culture too – are a symptom of decay, a deviation from the genuine, matter-of-course life of Nature.

Morality therefore makes man unnatural and artificial. He has to force himself in all kinds of ways, and cannot live his life in a natural way. He is pompous and affected, and stands on tip-toe. One cannot progress in this manner. The more self-confidence such a man has, the more loathsome and hypocritical he becomes. For DAO he is like the useless waste one throws out of one's kitchen or a festering boil, and all creatures hate him. Morality is simply a means of making most men feel self-important, so that they enjoy shining before other men. These mass-men feel clever and wise; dressed in the scanty mantle of their morality they are in high spirits, and feel only spite and condemnation for outsiders.

Lao Zi represents a turning point in the history of Chinese thought. He dissolved the laws, and placed ethics on a completely new basis. Confucius completely adopted Lao Zi's principal standpoint: for non-action, that is, not acting in accordance with laws and commandments, was also his ideal. For him too the natural, the instinctive, is the highest value. Only his method is different; and in his system the various concepts are ranked quite differently. Whereas for Lao Zi custom is a despicable exterior husk, for Confucius it is the means by which the individual can be led towards the good; and man's proper place within the organic context of mankind is provided by the subtle force of tradition, public opinion and fashion. Confucius also values the natural very highly; however, for him the natural is not the opposite but the harmonious complement of the human. Where Lao Zi separates nature and culture, Confucius unites them.

If we now ask the question 'How is man to find his position in the great context of nature?', we will begin to understand one of the most important concepts of the *Dao De Jing* – though it is still not as important as the concept of DAO itself. This is the concept of DE. The term DE stands at the beginning of section 38, a section which marks the beginning of the second part of Lao Zi's work. As we have already seen, this is one of the reasons the text has been called the *Dao De Jing*. Lao Zi gave the term DE a meaning quite different from the one it otherwise had in the Chinese language. The word is made up of the conceptual images of 'straightness' and 'heart', and originally meant 'that which proceeds straight from the heart' – the original life-force. In Chinese commentaries it is defined as 'that which beings receive in order to live'. For Lao Zi it is therefore 'life in its original force', flowing from DAO. DAO is the universal principle, DE refers to 'limitation'. It is the part which the individual has in DAO. This relationship is rather like certain Indian meditations on Brahman as the root of the world, and Atman as the root of the individual being, which is at the same time identical with the root of the world. For Lao Zi the word DE means something spontaneous, original or primal, that which is timeless and infinite in every individual living being. The Chinese language of later times, however, particularly in non-Daoist usage, has applied it far more abstractly. In these later times, it has come to signify 'the quality of something', and can be good or evil; it also means 'character that is to be fostered'; 'good character', 'virtuous conduct', and 'virtue'. DAO and DE have also often been translated as 'way' and 'virtue', in conjunction with the Confucian concepts of love and justice (*ren* and *yi*). No special emphasis is needed to show that the gradual trivialisation of the term (rather like the history of the German word for 'virtue') is absent from Lao Zi's use of it. I have therefore translated the word as 'Life'.

Life, in its highest manifestation, appears in the form of an individual personality; but the personality is, in a manner of speaking, only the vessel whose content is DAO. It wants nothing for itself, it does not even know itself. It does not act, has no goals and no designs; and just because of this, it lives. As soon as this unconsciousness is sullied or spoiled, the gradual downward path begins. The first step is towards love of one's fellowman, as yet with no goals or designs, 'not wanting anything', but nevertheless acting and being effective. The next step is towards justice, which means acting upon the principle *do ut des* and with goals and designs. The final step is morality: here one acts and if no one responds one waves one's arms about and resorts to force in order to subject men to a system of morality. Men, too, correspond to these levels: the lowest among men hardly know that the highest exist; the next ones down they love; the next ones further down they fear; and the next ones down from them they despise. Life, however, has no need to hanker after recognition. It is recognised without any fuss, for it engenders, nourishes, increases, fosters, completes, keeps and protects all beings. It creates without taking possession; it is effective without holding on to anything; it fosters without dominating: herein lies the secret of Life.

This Life is beyond the opposites of the phenomenal world, and unites them. Strong and glorious in itself, it remains calm in weakness or shame, without trying to work its way out of these. Its unrestricted effect springs from just this contrast between the treasure itself and the lowly garment of the treasure's bearer. And because of this it retains its accumulated force, which would otherwise be consumed in one-sided striving. This force renews itself all the time. While it does not provoke any resistance, it is nevertheless always capable of performing whatever activity any given moment requires. Whoever holds Life in hand in this way is like an infant who faces even the greatest perils without guile and safe in itself, and sustains even the greatest effort without tiring. Therefore whoever has this Life has no egotism, desires nothing for himself. He has no heart of his own but makes the heart of the people his heart. In other words he does to people not only what he wants them to do to him, but what the people wish him to do to them. His life is so powerful that before it all earthly opposites disappear. To good men he is good; and to non-good men he is also good: for Life is goodness. For him there are no 'lost causes' among men. Good men are important to him as teachers, evil men as those who are to be taught, so that he has use for both and can treat each on his own terms.

Although Life is individual in appearance, it is not limited to the individual. That which lives in me also lives in others. Thus I can see and understand others out of my own person, family, region, country and realm. This approach, in which one draws conclusions about others from oneself is also important in Confucianism. Lao Zi, however, takes it even further than the Confucians do. Where Confucius holds that one must respond to life with life, and to anger with correctness, Lao Zi says: 'Respond to anger with Life.' And he gives his reasons: 'If great anger is resolved there still remains a residue of anger.' As soon as the person who is offended takes his revenge, the burden of guilt shifts, in a manner of speaking, from the shoulders of the offender to the shoulders of the offended. Therefore the Man of Calling who knows Life takes upon himself the whole burden of duty – without burdening the other person. This, of course, requires strength: only the man who is bound up with Life will have shoulders strong enough to allow him to take the whole burden of duty upon himself and demand nothing of the other. Whoever does not have this Life insists on keeping up appearances, and puts the onus on the other in every case.

Through this non-quarrelling, Life continually gains new strength for it does not use up its strength in fighting against alien things which disturb it. To non-quarrelling belongs non-action. Life grows but it does nothing. 'Doing', 'consciously influencing events', 'efforts of will' – whatever the struggle of the world of appearances, the surface world of consciousness, may be called, all these only defuse states of tension in the short term. If one has ten goals per day and achieves all ten goals, one will exhaust oneself in the pettiness of daily routine, and will have no depth. The cosmic powers that are at every man's disposal are used up in all the unimportant movements which lead from birth to growing strength, and from there to rigidity and ultimately death. 'Wriggling about, growing stiff, and getting stuck in shallow meaninglessness' – this is the fate of the 'doers'. But Life itself does nothing, and yet nothing remains not done. For by relaxing and allowing itself to be permeated by DAO, Life develops limitlessly and reaches into the mysterious cosmic depths.

This produces a very definite attitude to things and events in man. He stands back, remains below, is content, humble, simple, modest. This weakness and softness is true strength, for it is the quality of all Life. What is hard and rigid is given over to death; what is soft and weak belongs to Life. Therefore does Lao Zi say about his three treasures: 'The first is called kindness; the second is called modesty; the third is called "Not daring to stand out in front in the world": for through kindness one can be brave, through modesty magnanimous, and through not daring to stand out in front one can be the leader of the skilled, and the specialists among men.'

This standing back in modesty confers that 'limitation' upon outward behaviour which saves time and energy. Whoever practises this 'limitation' need not expend time and energy unnecessarily. Therefore he will always have the time and energy at his disposal to tackle tasks in good time, when the seeds of future events have not yet entered the phenomenal world. He plans the difficult while it is still easy; and he works upon that which has not yet entered into appearance. This working in good time – a common feature in the philosophies of both Confucius and Lao Zi – is the secret of success. Men usually approach things when they are nearly completed, and in this way spoil everything. But the man who saves energy and time heaps up Life twofold; therefore there is nothing he can not deal with, and men do not know his limits. And just through this, he can have an effect upon them and possess the nourishing and stimulating powers they need.

The man who is permeated by the powers of the secret Life is the Man of Calling. The concept of a Man of Calling (*sheng ren*) is one that is shared both by Confucius and Lao Zi. This is the man whose mind is open to cosmic events and their laws. Whatever he experiences in the mysterious depths of his superconscious, life permeates all he does. This living experience confers magic upon his language and thought. Through his relatedness to the DAO of the world, the Man of Calling has the power to shape the world. But for this very reason he appears to stand back. For it is from this secret, in its seclusion, that the supernatural powers of essence flow.

Seen from this point of view the personal life of Lao Zi becomes clear. On the one hand he was a mystic, who expanded his Self so that it became the Self of the world, and who had had the great 'sight' of unity. From this sight the cloud-formations of his words were born, in constant flow like the ring of clouds that carried Faust over the abysses: they transform themselves into idealised forms, now of Helen of Troy, now of Gretchen. But Lao Zi is also a magician. Few have looked as deeply as he did into the weaving of universal forces, and revealed the principle by which one can have these forces at one's disposal – provided, of course, that one has learned to renounce one's ego, for it would be in dreadful danger once these forces were unleashed.

Comparison with Faust is both obvious and useful. Faust too makes a false start by trying to lay direct hold of what is beyond reach, by seeking to attain the unattainable. Catastrophe results; and only then is the two-fold way leading upwards unveiled to us: on the one hand, pure contemplation of the perceptibly beautiful, the way of affirmation of this world; on the other hand, the way of action stemming from inner experience. This too proves a dead end, but even in physical blindness Faust is vouchsafed a vision of the eternal female that 'leads us ever upwards', the way leading to the world beyond. When Faust yokes and utilises the satanic powers, his actions, gross and temporal, are those of the Titan of the West. Lao Zi's supra-sensual action is that of one who hearkens to Nature in her secret workings, one who can create without tools: it is the 'action' of the magician of the East.

5 STATE AND SOCIETY

Among the most radical of Lao Zi's statements are those sections in the *Dao De Jing* in which he criticises contemporary political and social conditions. Here he pursues the revolutionary current of the preceding centuries. 'The people are hungry because the upper classes devour too much in tax revenue: for this reason the people go hungry. The people are difficult to lead because the upper classes want to interfere too much: for this reason the people are difficult to lead. The people take death too lightly because the high and mighty seek too luxurious a life: for this reason the people take death so lightly.' With these words Lao Zi criticises the conditions in the state and society of his time. If it is really the case that people face death regardless of whether they do their work peacefully or whether they rise up in dangerous revolt, then they will not of course be worried about dying, and will choose the shorter way to destruction. As it is said in the *Book of Songs*: 'Had I known that this would be my lot, better that I had never been born.'

According to Lao Zi the reason such conditions arise in a state is that government meddles too much in the affairs of the citizens. The more things there are to avoid, the poorer people become; the more laws and decrees, the more thieves and robbers there will be. For all this meddling by government in the private lives of individuals brings about unrest and causes a great deal of damage. It is absolutely impossible to improve conditions by means of compulsion and brute force. The tortured populace will meet brute force with passive resistance and, ultimately, with revolution. Meanwhile, everything may well look as though it is flourishing. But this kind of flourishing carries the seed of decay within itself. The great boulevards may be beautiful and smooth, but the people take the side roads. The court may be rich and glittering, but weeds grow in the fields and the barns are empty. The garments of the upper classes are rich and beautiful, and everyone carries a rapier. Eating and drinking habits become refined. Goods abound. Where DAO should rule the land, robbers rule. However, inevitably, counter-DAO soon comes to an end.

Even outstanding individuals are unable to help in these circumstances. Confucius takes the same view. For him too it is a hopeless undertaking to try and create order by force and by law. Confucius is also against the lifelessness of public institutions and state interference in private affairs. But from this point onwards, the two philosophers hold characteristically different views. For Confucius culture, as such, is something precious. It is important for him to keep culture alive, to strengthen the forces that sustain and enliven the cultural organism and to fend off the forces which disturb, mechanise, profane and thereby destroy it. Therefore Confucius constructs a system of tensions and relationships. 'High and low', as the principle of social order, must be strengthened by custom and morality. Relationships must be arranged in such a way that everybody is in one respect an authority – even if only in the family circle – while in another respect he is subject to an authority above him. This explains why Confucius places such importance on morality. For him these relationships of tension are only the sources of power for the regulation of society. The upper classes have, in any case, higher duties, and are responsible for the influence they exercise through the force of example and inner attitude. This influence must be made possible: hence the social order. This influence must be exercised: hence the responsibility of the leaders.

Lao Zi is much more radical in this respect. For him culture and the edifice of the state have no value of their own. They function best if and when they are not noticeable at all. When a truly great man rules, people hardly know he exists. Works are accomplished, jobs are done, and all the people think of themselves as free. Thus freedom, self-reliance, is the fundamental principle of Lao Zi's order of the state. Letting people have their way, letting them do things, non-interference, non-governing: this is the highest goal. For if nothing is 'done', everything will be done of its own accord. Thus non-action is Lao Zi's fundamental principle. The reforms he suggests are, in the first place, purely negative: everything that is praised as morals and culture, conventional saintliness, knowledge, morality, duty, art and profit – is to be thrown overboard forthwith. For these are nothing but illusion, nothing but names invented by men and then held in high esteem, arrangements which everybody praises but which no longer represent any reality. This whole system of conventional lies produces nothing but sham, designed to obscure a bleak and desolate reality. All evil comes from a pathological overgrowth of knowledge. For, as we have already seen, a knowledge of 'names' represents things that do not exist. This arouses desire. The more difficult it is to obtain the things that have come to be known and respected in this way, the fiercer desire becomes. Next, men begin to fight for these things and robbery, theft, and murder follow. It is fantasy that deludes men: colours, sounds, tastes, games, rare treasures

– all these blinding appearances drag men's hearts away from the true depths of reality, and are the source of selfishness and delusion.

Therfore, if one genuinely wants to improve conditions, one must eradicate delusion. But delusion among the people can only be eradicated if the leaders take the lead in this: by not cherishing goods that are difficult to obtain, by being plain in their own requirements, by avoiding pomp, ceremony and all haughtiness, and by carrying themselves humbly and quietly among the people – in other words, by ignoring their ego and, in a sense, disappearing from the surface, so that they can be all the more comprehensively effective in their relationship with the forces of the deep. And so if the leaders of society were to put away what is distant and illusory and hold on to what is near and real it would be an easy matter to set the people aright. If one's goal is power and wealth, then of course one must foster enlightenment and knowledge among the people; then of course one will need all kinds of tools and machines to produce the goods – the profusion of which will benefit the upper classes alone. These means of 'improvement', machines and weapons (Lao Zi calls them collectively 'sharp implements') are, however, the harbingers of disorder. For this reason they must not be used. The path that Lao Zi points leads back from civilisation to Nature, from the 'enlightenment' of the people to simplicity. Wherever desires are aroused, wherever knowledge raises its head, they must be quelled by unutterable simplicity. And those who have knowledge must be prevented from achieving prominence.

However, this idyll of a calm people living in peace with Nature must be complemented with a care for their well-being. The people will avoid the delusions of fantasy of their own volition provided their physical circumstances are satisfactory. A wise government therefore looks after the people's well-being, and ensures that their food is healthy and plentiful, their dwellings are calm and peaceful, and their lives cheerful and happy. The Man of Calling cares for the people's bellies, makes sure that they are well-fed and have strong bones. Only then will their hearts become empty, that is, free of desire and dissatisfaction.

A great realm must be led in the same way as one fries small fish: one must not remove the scales; one must not shake them;

one must treat them with tenderness and calm. In this way Men will once again find their place in the peaceful state of Nature from which they have been torn by delusion.

These thoughts of Lao Zi have always played an important part in Chinese intellectual and spiritual life during times of political upheaval and social unrest. 'The Well in the Peach-Blossom Forest' of the poet Tao Yuan-Ming depicts a Utopian land, deep inside a mountain cave at the end of the world, which has always been free of the storms and ravages of the world, and has preserved its idyllic calm (see note to section 80, p. 142); and ever since, people have longed for this country in times of turmoil.

Nevertheless, at this point Lao Zi is faced with a severe problem. A return to Nature is very impressive as a sentimental construct of the imagination. But is it possible? To be sure, it was possible in Lao Zi's own time, when China was a relatively sparsely populated agricultural country. At that time it was considered a blessing if a state had a large population, and the ability to attract as many immigrants as possible from neighbouring states by means of its own well-ordered conditions. Things are different when the population increases beyond a certain point, and this creates demands on the production of the means of existence which can no longer be satisfied by primitive forms of craft or agriculture. Lao Zi does not suggest that man should return to Nature so that he would have to live from hand to mouth like an animal. He does, however, want man to be placed in an environment which he can control, and in which he can dwell calmly and contentedly, without losing his connection with the providing forces of the universe by chasing after unattainable things.

Seen from this angle, we can discover in Lao Zi's teaching a point of view that can be freely applied at any period in time, and in all possible economic circumstances. The decisive element is that men must always dominate the means that sustain their lives, and must not bury or block the sources of life in order to survive in the physical world. It is therefore perfectly possible to think, in the spirit of Lao Zi, of a machine culture in which machinery is handled in as matter-of-fact a way as agricultural implements were in ancient times; a society in which men can live in peace and security as the calm masters, and not the slaves of their machines. For the only devices Lao Zi condemns are the 'sharp implements', that is, things which are not mastered in such as way as to leave the mind completely free. It must, however, be emphasised here that Lao Zi did not pronounce these thoughts himself. His ideal is exclusively an idyllic existence of a primitive kind. Yet the thoughts just mentioned are distinctly in line with the ideals he stood for; for it is one of Lao Zi's convictions that the ideal of one era can in no way be a yardstick for another, and that every age must find its own means of living in a balanced and harmonious way.

The section which deals with transcendental forces is of particular interest. In complete harmony with his own times, Lao Zi assumes the existence of such forces, which, ringing out from the past, dominate and excite men as 'collective souls'. A true government also approaches this in a peaceable manner. The souls of the departed do not wander about as ghosts, that is their power does not harm men, does not cause division and partisanship. The residues of the past do not cause men to fight with one another, whether on religious or partisan grounds, and men face one another without harm.

Lao Zi pays equal attention to the organisation of social life, and to the shaping of political relations between different states. Like Confucius he assumes a hierarchic order of organisms. In the Confucian *Great Learning* (*Da Xue*) these are: person, family, state, mankind. Lao Zi adds one intermediate level: person, family, community, state, mankind. For him, therefore, the state is not the ultimate level, but a necessarily corporate part of mankind. Within mankind individual states are related to one another like the individual communities within a state. From this he draws a direct conclusion: absolute condemnation of any war of aggression.

Even the most beautiful weapons are instruments of doom, not instruments for the noble. The noble man uses them only if there is no alternative. Calmness and peace are his highest values. He is victorious but he does not rejoice in victory. Whoever would rejoice in victory would rejoice in the murder of men. Lao Zi looked deeply into the anatomy of war. He knew that wars do not begin with the declaration of war, and nor do they end with a peace treaty. He also knew that wars should be avoided before they even begin – not by means of a frantic build-up of arms, but by the removal of the causes of a possible war. He knew that one must bear the consequences after the fighting has ended. For where soldiers have passed thorns and thistles grow. Where great armies have been, bad times are certain to come. Therefore when order reigns on earth, racehorses are used to cart manure. When order is absent from the earth war-horses are bred in the fields outside the capital. In Lao Zi's view, war is permissible only in defence against an enemy's attack. Even in this case, one should only seek a decision, nothing more. For only by such restraint, which avoids the swing of the pendulum in the opposite direction, can peace be created. Lao Zi uses this principle of conducting war, which wins victory by retreat, as a parable for the right kind of action in other areas as well. However the clues given in these parables have subsequently been elaborated into a system for warfare which achieved a great deal of fame in China.

In Lao Zi's view, wars can be avoided through a correct relationship between states. Not surprisingly, he condemns all desire for conquest: for all conquest is based on an essential error, and lasting power has never been created by conquest. The purpose of the state is much rather – in fact, only – to enable the people who live within its borders to live their lives. Lao Zi's guidelines for communication between nations develop out of this principle. In his view, there are two forms of state: the male and the female. The female form of state is the one which keeps still, 'keeps itself below', and is 'saturated'. If these states understand their task correctly, they can be the means for the unification of the world; for the female wins victory over the male by its stillness. This process of mutual assimilation does, of course, also depend on the male states, that is, the small and active ones. The principle of fostering only genuine requirements, without hollow glory or a loud-mouthed appetite for conquest, applies to them too. These small states do, however, need expansion. This can be achieved just as well by coming together in peaceful union as it can be by war and subjection.

Most important of all are the attitudes and actions of the great realm or empire. It must 'keep itself below'. It will win smaller states over by uniting and nourishing them. To some extent China has proved this truth time and time again, throughout its history. Up till now [1910] it has assimilated every one of the aggressive, conquest-minded tribes which penetrated it from the periphery, through sheer size and 'stillness'. Obviously, Lao Zi's way of looking at things is fundamentally different from what has emerged in Western history. In the West nationalism and imperialism set the key notes. There was a similar phase in the East, just during Lao Zi's own time. The state of Qin Shi Huang Di was the prime example of this kind of political formation. But Lao Zi's thoughts have found their way into Chinese politics so that nowadays mankind has rather more ambivalent views on the subject. It is interesting to observe how the battle of ideas is being lived out in our time. The spirit of the West no longer simply knocks on China's doors from the outside; instead China itself has become the battleground for a confrontation between the different views of life.

6 DAOISM AFTER LAO ZI

Lao Zi's work has had an enormous influence on Chinese philosophy and on Chinese life. This influence did not come about all at once, but developed and increased gradually. An exposition of some of Lao Zi's views can already be found in the *Analects* of Confucius, in part agreeing with them, in part modifying them. Meng Zi, a representative of Confucianism at the end of the fourth century BC, does not mention Lao Zi anywhere, although he is critical of several of his successors. It is only in the collection of writings about the customs which originated in the time of the Han dynasty – but which can in fact be traced back to much older sources of various ages – that Lao Zi is mentioned several times as a man from whom Confucius took advice.

In spite of the fact that there are so few direct references to him, we find that Lao Zi's teaching did have a growing influence on the formation of Confucian thinking and teaching. In *The Great Learning* and in *Measure and Mean* (both of which, according to tradition, are earlier than Meng Zi, even though modern Chinese research dates them as later than that) one finds the metaphysical foundation of a Confucian social structure which gives glimpses in many places of an intellectual dialogue with Lao Zi. As for Daoist literature, there are works by alleged disciples of Lao Zi, like the one by the gatekeeper of the Xian Gu mountain pass, Guan Yin Xi, to whom Lao Zi is said to have left the *Dao De Jing*. However, these works are almost certainly products of a later era, as are many writings – some in the form of Buddhist sutras, for example – which mention Lao Zi or Lao

Hun, or Tai Shang Lao Jun as he was called in later times, as their originator.

We must not, however, consider Lao Zi in isolation. He belongs among the 'hidden sages' who played such an important part in Confucius's later life. In those circles views like Lao Zi's were fairly common. But this is not the first time that these thoughts appeared. They are secret teachings that have been handed down from ancient times. This is borne out by the later saga which praises 'the Yellow Emperor' (Huang Di) as the founder of Daoist views. We have already pointed out that there are quotations from these older adages in the *Dao De Jing*. In some cases, their names are the only traces left of these sages, as for instance the master Hu Kin Lin, or his disciple Po Hun Wu-Jen. In others, legend provides us with some details, in particular about Lie Yu-Kou, from who we have a work in eight volumes under the name of Lie Zi. This man is also specifically mentioned by the philosopher Zhuang Zi (*c.* 335-275 BC), not as a legendary figure but as a real person who had, however, been so magnified by legend that supernatural and miraculous powers were attributed to him.

It would be very pleasing if we did have an authentic work from the fourth or fifth century BC before us in the work of Lie Zi. However this is not the case. We cannot date the compilation of this book any earlier than the fourth century AD. Nevertheless, the book is based on older material. Lie Zi develops Lao Zi's teaching by giving it a stronger metaphysical emphasis. His thinking deals with the antinomies of space and time, with the evolutionary problems of various species of living beings, and with several similar issues. Its naturalism is, however, more pronounced and narrowly applied than the *Dao De Jing*. DAO is increasingly presented as a metaphysical substance which brings about all becoming and passing away, and which projects itself into the phenomenal world without itself ever becoming phenomenal. It is characteristic that many stories are told in the form of parables; some of these are miracle stories, designed to show the power of a practice of yoga which is directed towards unification. In Lie Zi we find the magical element being developed side by side with the mystical.

Yang Zhu, however, is a historical personality. At the time of the Confucian Meng Zi his teaching had already attracted such a circle of disciples and followers that Meng Zi counted him among his main adversaries. He attacked Yang Zhu for his egotistical views which, he thought, rejected and dissolved all relations in the state and between states. He would not give a hair from his head to benefit the world: this showed a selfishness which made it impossible for men to live together. However, we do not learn from Meng Zi what the real attraction in the teaching of Yang Zhu was, for he had almost as many followers as Confucius and Mo Di (the third great philosopher besides Lao Zi and Confucius in the sixth century BC). But in the book of Lie Zi we have an exposition of the teaching of Yang Zhu which is a welcome complement to Meng Zi's account. According to Lie Zi, Yang Zhu was a disciple of Lao Zi who had not fully understood the latter's teaching but had developed it in a one-sided manner. In this respect Lao Zi suffered much the same fate as Confucius. Just as the teachings of Confucius were at first turned by the main branch of his school into a one-sided and more or less narrow-minded ritualism, so Lao Zi's teaching was turned into a one-sided and thus restricted naturalism. In Zhuang Zi we find a tale (book VII, 4) in which Yang Zhu seeks instruction from Lao Zi. He asks whether a man who is keen and strong, who has penetrating powers of reasoning and an ever-present sense of clarity, who is untiring in his search for DAO – whether such a man could be put on the same level as the wise kings of ancient times. Lao Zi rebukes him in rather rough terms, and then continues: 'The works of the wise kings were such that they filled the whole world with them, and yet it did not look as if they came from them. They formed all beings and gave them presents, and the people were not aware of it. They stood in the immeasurable and walked in non-existence.'

Here we see Yang Zhu as a disciple of Lao Zi. But we also see a deviation from Lao Zi's true standpoint in his essentially intellectual approach. This manner suits the stories and speeches that are recounted in the seventh book of Lie Zi very well. These passages reveal him to be a ruthlessly sharp-witted thinker. He profiles Lao Zi's views on letting-go and non-action, in other words the complete assimilation of man into the context of Nature. But he lacks Lao Zi's kindness and breadth, and therefore his views appear extreme. All activity is rejected. A pessimistic fatalism pours a caustic fluid over the whole of life. The strongly-flavoured libation leaves a bitter after-taste. Everything is totally vain. Good and evil are completely unimportant, as are all other differences between men. It goes without saying that from his point of view everything to do with life in society is absurd, that every attempt to organise the state or even participate in public life must be rejected from the outset. Consistent egotism, fatalism and pessimism are all that remains for him of Lao Zi's rich world. But it is understandable that it was precisely the extremism and frivolity of his views that found acclaim and became fashionable among a drowning generation. There is no doubt that Yang Zhu has been effective as a dissolving agent in the Chinese thought of that time because of his freedom from all ties. One understands how Meng Zi saw a creeping poison in his views, one which had to be eliminated if mankind was not to disintegrate.

It is Zhuang Zi, a younger contemporary of Meng Zi, who really brought Lao Zi's teaching into Chinese philosophy. Zhuang Zi is a splendid figure in Chinese intellectual and spiritual life. He is the poet among Chinese philosophers of the fourth century BC, and his influence on later poetry in the south of China has been as strong as it has on subsequent philosophy. Hardly anything is known about his life. The few biographical features that one can gather from his work tell us no more than that he led an essentially inner life while living in outward poverty. He consistently rejected invitations from princes to join their courts as an adviser, and turned away the messengers who brought him these propositions rather roughly. On the other hand he did not withdraw from the world, but lived as the head of a family under rather constrained conditions, and not without occasional financial difficulties. He was quite definitely in touch with the intellectual currents of his time. He was in contact with the Confucian school, although not with its orthodox branch but with another group which has made important contributions to Confucian tradition. He had the greatest respect for Confucius the Master, particularly after the great turning point Confucius experienced in his sixtieth year; and we learn much that is of great value from Zhuang Zi about this intellectual and spiritual turning point. Zhuang Zi also had connections with the philosopher Hui Shi, who made a name for himself as a dialectician and politician. Hui Shi seems to have been close to the so-called 'school of sophists' in central China. Nothing of importance has been preserved from his rather numerous writings. But from Zhuang Zi we learn quite a bit about his views. He seems to have devoted himself mainly to logical distinctions. Zhuang Zi had many disputations with him, probably more as an exercise in dialectics than in the hope of converting him.

But of all these links and associations with other philosophers – links not without influence on Zhuang Zi's thinking – the influence of Lao Zi stands out above all others. Zhuang Zi puts forward not only a Daoist worldly wisdom but a true Daoist philosophy. His fundamental philosophical views are found in the first seven books of his writings, the so-called 'inner section'; the rest are subsidiary and supplementary. The first book is called 'Walking in leisure'. It is an exposition of the whole work. Earthly life with its fates and influences is compared to a small quail darting through the brushwood, while 'Life', in blessed serenity is free of all pettiness. It is also compared to the great bird Peng whose wings appear like hanging clouds in the sky when it begins its flight from the southern to the northern ocean. The second book, 'On the balancing of world views', is of particular importance. Here Zhuang Zi offers solutions to contemporary controversies from the Daoist point of view. His time was one of a great battle of ideas. The ancient, religiously founded world view had collapsed long ago. All kinds of ideas, often diametrically opposed to each other, had arisen in its place, and confronted one another in a dialectical battle. Taking the line of the *Dao De Jing*, Zhuang Zi realised the inevitably conditioned limits of all these opposing views, fighting battles of logic with one another. None of these views would be proved right. Zhuang Zi found a way out of this by switching from disputation to intuition, whereby a unified view of essence is achieved. This second book begins with a great rhapsody on the music of the heavenly organ; and ends with the enigmatic parable of the dream of the butterfly, in which life and dream confront one another as two different realms, and no one can say which is real and which is unreal. In his third book he offers a practical application of his insight. The task is to find the Lord of Life; not to strive for a particular individual situation but to follow the main arteries of life, and be content with the external situation one is in. For it is not a change of external conditions that can save us, but a different attitude to existing conditions of life as derived from DAO. This gives us access to a world beyond differences.

The subject of Zhuang Zi's fourth book is the world of men in society rather than of individual human life. It shows the way in which one can be effective in the social and political world. Here too it is important to maintain a comprehensive standpoint, and not tie oneself up in 'expertise'. 'Expertise' or specialisation can be useful, but this very usefulness can cause one to be used. One can become caught in the web of the phenomenal world, like a wheel in the large machinery of society, but precisely because of this, one becomes a 'professional', a one-sided expert, while the 'unusable' man, who stands above all opposites, thereby saves his life.

His fifth book deals with the 'Seal of complete life'. It shows in several parables how an inner connection with DAO provides a true life without designs, and exercises an inner influence upon Men before which all external insufficiencies must vanish. He relates stories of cripples and men of extreme ugliness who demonstrate this truth most clearly contrary to external appearances. The contrast between this inner resource or treasure and the sack-cloth garment of outward appearance is thus brought all the more clearly into focus. This is a feature of Daoism which has given it a somewhat paradoxical quality even in later times. This theme can also be traced in fairy tales where a powerful magician or a saving god appears as a beggar clothed in rags, derelict and covered in dust on some street corner. It is easy to see that this view bears a certain resemblance to the Christian 'scandal of the cross'. For in Christianity too, humility and self-denial are shown as the way to elevation and blessedness. However, there is also a great difference between the two. In Christian terms this elevation, glory and blessedness, the one side of the paradox, is the goal that is longed for. Suffering and lowliness are only the means towards this end. Christianity tends to see the path of suffering within the short span of our time on earth as the purchase price for a glory beyond measure, and of unlimited duration. For Daoism, however, lowliness or ugliness is no longer something that must be suffered. It is not a state one would wish to exchange for another. Instead, once a man has attained the comprehensive view of essence, he is beyond the opposites of happiness and unhappiness, life and death altogether, none of which come anywhere near Dao. For these opposites are equally necessary links in an eternally transforming cycle. It would be wrong to exclude any one pole permanently and eternalise its opposite. In the first place this would be impossible, and in the second it would mean that one would still be beholden to the phenomenal world.

When Hui Shi asked Zhuang Zi whether there really were men without human feelings, the latter answered with an unconditional 'Yes'. Hui Shi then said: 'Such a man without human feelings cannot be called a man.' Zhuang Zi replied: 'Since the eternal Dao of Heaven has given him human form it must be possible to call him a man.' Thereupon Hui Shi: 'But feelings are part of the concept of "man".' Zhuang Zi replied: 'These are not the feelings I have in mind. When I say that someone is without feelings I mean that such a man does not harm his inner essence by inclinations and disinclinations. He follows Nature in all things and does not actively seek to increase his life.' Then Hui Shi asked: 'If he does not actively seek to increase his life, how can his essence persist?' And Zhuang Zi replied: 'The eternal DAO of Heaven has given him his form, and he does not harm his inner essence by inclinations and disinclinations. But you occupy your mind with things that are outside it and vainly engage your life forces . . . Heaven has given you your physical form, and you know nothing better than to repeat your sophistries.' (Book V, 6.)

Zhuang Zi's sixth book, 'The Great Ancestor and Master', is also very important. It deals with what happens when men find access to the great ancestor, DAO. 'True men did not fear loneliness. They had accomplished no heroic deeds and made no plans. Therefore they had no reason for regret when they failed and no reason for exultation when they succeeded. Therefore they were able to climb the highest peaks without getting dizzy; they could walk through water without getting wet; they could walk through fire without getting burned. They had no dreams when they slept and no worries when they woke. Their food was simple, and they breathed easily and deeply. They did not know an extreme attachment to life nor fear of death; they did not complain about leaving life, nor rejoice about entering it. They came in serenity, and serene they went. They did not forget their origins and did not strive towards their end. They took what came to them joyfully and let go whatever went without giving it a further thought. This is called "Not impeding DAO by consciousness, and not trying to help what comes from Heaven by what is human".' In this way, even the profoundest issues of suffering and death are treated in the most sovereign manner.

The seventh book, 'For use by kings and princes', is the last in the series, and deals with ruling by non-ruling. It is said there: 'The highest of men uses his heart like a mirror. He does not run after things and does not walk towards them. He mirrors them but does not hold on to them.'

To sum up, then, Zhuang Zi develops Lao Zi's Daoism further, by using its methods in order to solve the philosophical problems of his own time. He clothes Lao Zi's teaching in the brilliant gown of poetic language, and formulates pointed parables which make the ineffable in Daoist concepts shine forth in flashes of lightning. With him the parable joins the paradox to make the ineffable approachable. Therefore in his epilogue he says of his method:

> Mostly I offer parables
> And many words from old sayings;
> From a well-filled cup a daily drink
> Just so that eternity's light may play upon it.

He also adheres closely to Lao Zi's thinking about the phenomenal world. He too lives in the depths of DAO, and the phenomenal world is a phantomlike dream to him. It does not matter whether he is Zhuang Zi or a butterfly: one is as much dream existence as the other. He lived his life hidden away, like his master. We do not know whether he had disciples. Nevertheless, it seems that a large part of what has been handed down in his name did not come directly from him, and so it is reasonable to assume that some kind of school existed. In any case, it is clear that he had an enormous influence on philosophy and literature. This is borne out by the fact that the term 'Lao Zhuang' – which combines the names of Zhuang Zi and Lao Zi – is often used to describe Daoist views. (In the same way, Lao Zi's affinity to antiquity is indicated by the term 'Huang Lao', where 'Huang' refers to Huang Di, 'the Yellow Emperor', venerated as the patron saint of Daoism, just as Yao and Shun are the patron saints of Confucianism.) The influence of the poet-philosopher Zhuang Zi is most apparent in the literature of the south. The world view of the poetry of Chu, which has enriched Chinese culture as a new art form from the Yangtse river basin, shows this influence clearly.

A peculiar outgrowth of Daoism can be found in the philosophy of Han Fei Zi. He was a prince from the ruling family of the state of Han, which was in great danger at this time. He tried to get a plan to save his country accepted by his government, but they would not listen to him. He then turned to the state of Qin in the west, which under its ruler Qin Shi Huang Di, had begun to usurp the rule of the whole empire by the destruction of all other states. Li Si was then the all-powerful minister in Qin. Earlier, Han Fei Zi had visited the classes given by the Confucian Xun Qing together with Li Si; the general opinion was that he was the more illustrious of the two friends. It is therefore understandable that the ruler of Qin, who already knew Han Fei Zi from his writings, was happy to make use of him for a time. The part played by Li Si is not quite clear. In any case, Han Fei Zi was imprisoned soon after his arrival in Qin, whether by design or with the acquiescence of Li Si. He committed suicide there in 233 BC, in order to escape a worse fate. His writings, however, were highly regarded in Qin after his death.

At this time influences from different cultural centres – northern Confucianism, southern Taoism and the central Chinese school of Mo Di – had already begun to merge with one another. A compilation like the Lü-Shi Chun-Qiu (*Spring and Autumn Annals* of Lü Bu-Wei) shows this new eclecticism at quite an early stage. It was no longer considered important to support one particular school of disputation or another; instead thoughts were taken from here and there according to what had come to common knowledge at the time. Han Fei Zi was not purely eclectic, but took up a unified standpoint which he supported with views from all schools. He took his central theme from the thought of the statesmen of central China. It was thought that order and the government of the state could be achieved through laws and political arrangements. This approach contradicted both Confucianism – which wanted to effect order not through correct laws but through correct men – and Daoism, whose highest aim was that no ordering arrangements should be made at all. The idea of a legal foundation for the state had evolved out of the views of Mo Di, but was also prevalent among the great statesmen of the era. The way in which the Confucian Xun Qing conceives morality as a means for creating order is also similar to this line of thinking. Han Fei

Zi took the strong emphasis on authority and the ruler's right from Confucianism, but developed this into a principle of absolute monarchy, stressing the importance of employing competent men. But all these thoughts are wrapped in certain Daoist principles. It is therefore quite understandable that he took to commenting expressly on, and collecting examples of Lao Zi's sayings.

As we have already seen, Lao Zi valued non-action above all as the best way of doing things, and taught that the highest and wisest of rulers were the ones who understood how to stand back to such an extent that the people were hardly aware of their existence. This non-action on the ruler's part is also emphasised by Han Fei Zi. But he imparts a different meaning to it. For Lao Zi non-action is the highest form of action, for through it the nature of the ruler comes into accord with cosmic influences, and in this way secretly co-operates with the necessity of a natural force. According to Lao Zi only an exceptionally great and magnanimous man – one who loves the world in himself – could practise this kind of rule through non-action. Han Fei Zi sees things quite differently. For him non-action is important for the comfort and safety of the ruler. Why should the ruler have to make any effort? All he has to do is choose competent and industrious officials. They will not cease in their efforts to do all the work for him, so that he can enjoy the happiness of his elevated position without having to make any effort himself. 'He does "non-action" and nothing remains not done.' This seems to be quite in accord with Lao Zi – but, of course, it only seems so.

There is yet another point. It is not only more comfortable for the prince to have his officials act for him, it is also safer. For if something goes wrong it will be the responsibility of those who did it, while the monarch himself will remain free of responsibility and in a position to punish his clumsy officials. One could well ask whether this account, which completely excludes the prince from the mechanics of government, is not simply aimed at providing a kind of *dolce vita* for the ruler, so that he will not disturb the business of state by his intervention; yet it becomes clear, in the end, that Han Fei Zi is offering his advice, in the manner of Machiavelli, to princes alone. This follows from the second principle he propounds. Lao Zi had said that one must not show the realm's sharp implements to the people just as one must not take the fish from the deep. What he meant was that one should keep the people in a state of simplicity and contentment, so that the peace of this great simplicity might not be disturbed by all kinds of political scheming or trickery. Han Fei Zi takes up this principle, but transforms it too, in characteristic manner. In his view, the ruler should always keep his state officials fully occupied and in suspense, without clear definition and in fear about their status, so that every one of them will fulfil his task as perfectly as possible. But he should always keep the final decisions to himself. He should be mysterious and invisible like a god, and unpredictable and sudden in meting out reward and punishment in order to enhance the attitudes which serve his purpose. In this way he keeps reward and punishment, as the levers of power, absolutely in his own hands and uses them to achieve his aims – which he never discloses. The power and terror that result from uncertainty, are the means which Han Fei Zi counsels the prince to use. Here we see Lao Zi's thought already distorted into a system of black magic.

This can also be seen in Han Fei Zi's views on human nature. For Lao Zi the origins of human nature were in harmony with the universe and its laws. Desire alone was the source of all evil, and had to be subdued. For Han Fei Zi, however, desire is the core of human nature. Of course, desire is evil from the beginning. And yet it must be nourished and fostered, for it is the only lever by which the prince can force men into his service. A man who desires nothing, who no longer fears anything, who no longer hopes for anything is useless to the prince; he is even dangerous. The best thing to do with him is to do away with him. All others must be thoroughly mistrusted. A prince must not trust his officials for they are his enemies: only by keeping them in suspense does he make them ready to serve him. But he must not trust his wife and his child either, for they might become tools in the hands of ambitious officials who will use them for their ends. Trust is the root of all evil. One must love men only as a means to an end. One loves a horse because it runs well. A king loves his subjects because they fight for him. One loves a doctor because he heals wounds and stops one losing blood. One must be cautious in one's love. A cartwright wishes people to be rich and refined, not because he does not begrudge them their wealth and refinement, but because he wants to sell them his carriages. A coffin-maker wants people to die not because he hates them, but because otherwise nobody would buy his coffins. In the same way a prince must always remain aware that his offspring will always wish for his death, not because they hate him but because the way that things are, they will benefit from his death. Therefore he must always behave cautiously towards men who would benefit from his death.

Han Fei Zi applies these principles cold-bloodedly to all matters of state. He derives an absolutely tyrannical policy of power from them. He allows no firm principles, because whatever benefits the prince in any situation must be done. Ruthless opportunism is the only principle worthy of an unprejudiced ruler. Laws must be strict, and they must function with unfailing certainty, mechanically, like the forces of nature. Only in this way will the prince remain above all responsibility; for it is not he who kills men but they who kill themselves when they get caught between the jaws of an automatically functioning penal machinery. No one should be allowed to be free within the state, except the prince himself. Nor should there be freedom of thought or speech. Only when the inclinations and views of the people are in complete accord with the prince's goals can the prince be certain of his people. For this reason love and pity on the part of a prince must be condemned, for these would introduce an element into government that would be incompatible with its mechanism. Only if and when that mechanism is flawless can it be truly effective.

Han Fei Zi turned Daoism into something strange and peculiar – although logically one can see how every one of his conclusions could be deduced from the words of Lao Zi. Han Fei Zi was a bold thinker who did not allow the machine-like structure of his thoughts to be disturbed by considerations of kindness, or motives of the heart. As I have already mentioned, this ice-cold consistency is something he has in common with Machiavelli. But it is fitting that this defender and teacher of tyrants of the world should meet his death in prison at the hands of his most eager disciple, Qin Shi Huang Di. His friend and fellow-traveller, Li Si, who helped to bring about his death – not because Han Fei Zi was more humane than Li Si, but because the latter felt that he could apply these principles better alone, as the only servant of his lord and master, rather than in his fellowship with such a competent companion – was himself cut in two not long after this by the son of the prince he had made emperor of the world, in gratitude for services rendered.

From this example, we can see how things had developed in China at the time of the collapse of its ancient civilisation. The beautiful, free world with its high heavens above, the calm, peaceful realm of DAO which Lao Zi had unveiled to the enchanted eye, had become a sinister inferno in which daemons had been let loose. Han Fei Zi's teaching is to the Daoism of Lao Zi what the Spanish *autos-da-fé* and the witch-hunts of the Middle Ages were to the gentle teaching of the Man from Nazareth in whose name they were executed.

Another encyclopaedia of Daoist teaching can be found in the works collectively known under the name *Huai-Nan-Zi*, after the time of Han Fei Zi. These writings can be traced to Liu An, the grandson of the Emperor Wu Di of the Han dynasty, who had been appointed prince of the district of Huai Nan. He was deeply devoted to Daoism and gathered a large number of scholars and magicians at his court. He had them make a compilation of Daoist knowledge which at first was called *Hong Lie Chuan (Notes on the Great Clarity)*, but was later given the title *Huai-Nan-Zi*. Liu An spent his fortune on alchemical experiments, and later became involved in a political intrigue which was meant to secure the succession to the imperial throne for him. However, the conspiracy was discovered and the prince committed suicide in 122 BC. Later Daoist writers, however, claimed that his disappearance from the world was due to the fact that he had succeeded in being accepted into the company of the immortals. His teaching reveals how the union of northern and southern thought had progressed, and how the strength of the waves from the central Chinese school of thought that had first given Han Fei Zi's views their clarity and precision, had faded away. By Liu An's time all the strategies for enslaving men and helping the tyrants' power had not only rebounded on their perpetrators, but everything they had achieved by helping the house of Qin to world domination had collapsed before long, and with it had gone the whole of ancient Chinese culture. It had exceeded the limits of its strength. Meanwhile the Han dynasty had surfaced. At first it gave free reign to the superstitions of popular religion, but then it discovered in Confucianism the most useful support for order in the state. In this way, Confucianism was given the position which it was to hold for some two thousand years afterwards, though not without considerable crises or changes in fortune.

The *Huai-Nan-Zi* compilation is an interesting attempt to unite Daoism and Confucianism. It too begins with DAO – which in name, at least, is as much the foundation of Confucianism as it is of Daoism, even though, as we have seen, the same term has a somewhat different meaning in the two schools. There is a hymnal glorification of the omnipotence and omnipresence of DAO in *Huai-Nan-Zi*, just as there had been in earlier Daoist writings. However, it is clear that it does not always reach the heights of the original teaching. Where Lao Zi's view of DAO is essentially qualitative, *Huai-Nan-Zi* emphasises the quantitative aspect. In addition, some of its comments suggest that DAO and the world belong together, that DAO is the omnipresent soul of the world and yet capable of being narrowed down by magic. The phenomenal world of individual differences and the world beyond appearances and individual differences begin to separate into a present world and a world beyond. No wonder, then, that the *Huai-Nan-Zi* compilation turns to magical means in order to pass from this world into the one beyond, or else drag what is beyond into this world and so achieve immortality or death-lessness. For under these circumstances one would want to hold on to having-been-born, to life in this world, without having to pay the price of death, of stepping out of life and the phenomenal world for it. The art of magic takes the place of this price. We shall have to come back to this problem when we consider magical Daoism. At this point, it is sufficient to draw attention to the fine cracks in the structure of the thought of the time through which these mists were able to penetrate.

The influence of the Confucian school as it is set forth in the metaphysics of *The Great Learning* and *Measure and Mean*, can be seen quite clearly in *Huai-Nan-Zi*, for it replaces the concept of DE, or Life – which to Lao Zi meant 'DAO become-individual' – by the Confucian concept of *xing* or nature, essence. Like DAO, the essence of man is calm and pure in its original state, and only becomes clouded and restless through contact with the objects that cause desires and emotions. In its purity the essence of man is one with DAO. This original pure essence dwells in man. It will be temporarily covered, just as the clouds cover the stars. It fluctuates just as the raging waves make the sky appear to fluctuate. But just as the polar star shows the seafarer the course he must take when the elements are in uproar, so man's innermost essence is his guiding star in the hustle and bustle of life.

According to *Huai-Nan-Zi*, it is easy to foster this essence; since it is originally good and spoiled only by reacting to external influences, it is enough to remove the external causes and man will right himself all of his own accord. However, the *Huai-Nan-Zi* compilation acknowledges desire as something that necessarily belongs to human nature, and that cannot be completely eliminated. Where desire is simply directed at the satisfaction of natural needs it is not harmful and need not be fought. Only when it chases after phantoms and causes man to 'get beside himself' is it an evil and must it be fought. But since goodness is engrained in the essence of man, he needs no effort and no action to become good: he simply has to obey his inner voice. Therefore it is easy to do what is good, but far more difficult to do evil because it contradicts Nature and causes man to pervert his own essence.

In order to avoid the excessive desires that would lead to evil, it is necessary to eliminate as far as possible the differences that exist between men with regard to possessions and pleasures. For if men no longer see desirable things in the possession of others they will not be drawn to envy or argument. The ideal world of *Huai-Nan-Zi* is constructed in such a way that simplicity rules as far as possible, so that general contentment may bring about happiness for all in society.

Considering the way in which the work has been compiled, it is not surprising that one finds certain contradictions in it. It assumes that goodness has a factual existence in Nature, so that it is only a question of setting it free by means of cultivation and education; but it also puts forward the view that good and evil are natural talents which are man's inheritance through fate. There are noble men who are good just because they cannot be otherwise; they need not learn or practise good, because it is engrained in their original essence. On the other hand there are those who cannot be improved by any amount of education and effort, because evil is engrained in their nature. These talents are as inescapable as a beautiful or an ugly face, which essentially cannot be changed no matter how much one tries. According to this view, education and culture can only influence the large mass of the mediocre who have talents for both good and evil. This contradiction between necessity (fate) and freedom is, of course, one that is very difficult to overcome, if it can be overcome at all. Confucius, too, once said that the loftiest saints and the lowliest fools could not be changed, although he also held that men are, by nature, close to one another and only the fleeting habits of fashion produce distances between them.

To sum up, then, we must say that the *Huai-Nan-Zi* compilation shows hardly any signs of independent thought. However, this eclectic work does have some merit because of the skilful way in which it brings the various trends of the preceding era into a unified and coherent system, giving pride of place to goodness wherever it finds it. The whole work has an aura of mildness and kindness, which is almost certainly an expression of the personality of the prince who had the work compiled by his scholars.

Huai-Nan-Zi marks the end of what may be termed the philosophically creative literature of Daoism. However, Daoism has influenced philosophers of other schools, just as Confucian influences can be found in Daoism after Zhuang Zi. Among the Confucian philosophers who based themselves to some extent on Daoist teaching were Dong Zhong-Shu and Yang Sheng, as well as the sceptic and materialist Wang Chong. The influence of Daoism on poets of the Confucian school is traceable even today. It has led the more thoughtful among statesmen, particularly during periods of political unrest, out of the political arena of the day and into the quiet mountains, or to the shores of the great ocean. But the tendency towards religious magic in Daoism has been even more influential than this, and has found its way into popular thought.

Classical Chinese philosophy is distinguished by a remarkable absence of superstition. There is hardly any classical literature of that period in human history which bypasses these lower depths with as much sovereign calm. It would, however, be wrong to assume that these lower depths had not existed among the people of China. They existed below and beside the philosophical heights, as is always the case when the thinking of a few rises up to purer spheres. This had to do with the unquiet times at the end of the classical period, for with the collapse of the ancient culture the lower strata came once more to the surface.

The conditions for this upsurge had been prepared by various elements. In the north, Confucianism had always emphasised ancestral cults. Confucius himself, however, was free of all superstition. For him ancestral cults were simply a religious form of the ordinary ethical duty of filial love after the death of one's parents. He never deliberately pronounced on whether or not the dead possessed consciousness. It was quite understandable that this solemn concern with death in burial rites and ancestral cults had its effects. What is more, a belief in ghosts which had not been previously associated with ancestral cults found a point on to which they could fasten in these cults. Thus popular beliefs developed a rich hierarchy of all kinds of gods and daemons, who were all thought of as somehow connected with the souls of men who had passed away. The teaching of Mo Di (who was otherwise distinctly inclined towards rationalism and utilitarianism) strengthened this trend by its resolute theism, and by its emphasis on belief in higher beings. The sophisticated sceptics and the massive materialists had no way of stemming the tide. Gods and daemons were happily revived.

But in the south, too, the intellectual and spiritual life showed signs of the new tendency. In Zhuang Zi one finds a great number of parables about adepts and 'true men', who come onto the stage as magicians, 'who do not drown even when the floods rise to the sky, and who do not become hot even in the midst of the fire that melts rocks and metal'. From this developed a belief in Daoist circles that it was possible during one's lifetime to escape the cycle of death and rebirth with one's physical body intact, and rise up to immortal life as a blessed spirit. It is clear that in Zhuang Zi we are dealing with a mystical experience which is the product of a sublime practice of yoga, 'when the heart becomes like dead ashes and the body like dry wood'. The tendency to embellish these supra-intellectual experiences, and project them into a colourful fairytale world of superstition, is, however, easy to understand.

In addition, a new philosophy originated by the scholar Zou Yan and his school developed a dynamic view of Nature which was based on the dual powers of light and darkness taken from the *Book of Changes*, and on the five states of transformation – the watery, the fiery, the metallic, the vegetal and the earthy – taken from the *Book of Records*; and this threw the gates wide open to a belief in miracles. Alchemical ideas appeared on the scene: one of Zou Yan's followers wanted to make use of the miraculous powers of nature in order to produce the 'Golden

Potion', the elixir of life that would impart immortality to the human body.

External circumstances favoured these views. Chinese culture originated in the basin of the Yellow River, and only during the time we are now looking at did it reach the area of the Yangtse River. There, however, it encountered not a savage tribe without culture, but another equally highly developed culture, albeit one that had quite different features. In the *Elegies* of Chu in particular we find figures from this mythology leading a colourful life, and from there these myths flow into Chinese literature in general. This movement spread towards the south, and finally reached the coast. Before this, ancient culture had been distinctly continental: now for the first time it touched a maritime sphere of influence. As in all maritime cultures, the myth of the sun now becomes a prominent feature, along with the myth of the sea. Tales of the Three Islands of the Blessed appear, islands that lie somewhere far in the eastern sea, inhabited by blessed spirits who have been freed of all earthly heaviness.

Daoism, itself close to the south, naturally adopted this new body of mythology with enthusiasm. It already contained a number of tendencies that inclined towards these myths. I mentioned Yang Zhu's pessimism and the otherworldliness of Zhuang Zi earlier in this commentary. These views were the starting points for imagining a better world beyond, a world that was waiting, somewhere lost in space, for the chosen who had fled from the battle fields of life, and who would there find peace.

The reason this trend permeated Chinese thought for several centuries was that a large number of Chinese princes of the pre-Christian centuries expressly encouraged it. The magicians who knew the secrets of this cult were called *fang shi*, roughly translatable as 'sorcerers'. They were welcome at the princely courts because the princes wanted to add physical immortality to their worldly power. Many a prince died of the strange medicinal brews that his court magicians prepared for him. It is a strange coincidence that the two most powerful rulers at the turn of the millennium were adherents of this kind of magical Taoism. Qin Shi Huang Di, having united the world under his rule, wanted to ascertain how long he would be able to enjoy his power. He summoned magicians from everywhere in great numbers. He then made a pilgrimage to the holy mountain in the east, the Taishan, and personally offered sacrifices to it; the god of this mountain, who rules over life and death, has played an important part in Daoism ever since. He also sent messengers into the eastern sea and a whole group of young people, male and female, sailed out into the uncharted ocean in order to discover the Islands of the Blessed. He gathered hundreds of sorcerers at his court to concoct the elixir of life.

The founder of the Han dynasty, too, was very favourably inclined towards Daoism. A number of his heroes and advisers – the mysterious Dong Fang Shuo, for example, who was considered a reincarnation of Lao Zi within a hundred years after his death, or his most faithful friend Zhang Liang (d. 189 BC) – were adherents of these forms of Daoist sorcery. The legend that developed around Zhang Liang is characteristic. In his youth he had met an extremely old man who was sitting down, and who had let one of his sandals fall from his foot. Zhang Liang reverently picked it up. At this, the old man asked him to come to a certain place five days later where he would impart an important revelation. When Zhang Liang arrived at this place, the old man was already there; he rebuked him for being late and asked him to come back another day. It was only on the third occasion that Zhang Liang succeeded in arriving in good time. Then the old man gave him a book which would make him the teacher of an emperor, and asked him to come back to the same place thirteen years later, when he would meet him again in the shape of a yellow stone (*huang shi*). This book gave Zhang Liang the wisdom with which he helped his lord and friend to success. When he returned to the same place thirteen years later he did indeed find a yellow stone, in which he recognised his old teacher.

A descendant of Zhang Liang, born in AD 34, was Zhang Dao-Ling. He was born near the Tian Mu Shan in what is now the province of Zhejiang, near the mouth of the Yangtse River. Early on he turned to the study of Daoist teaching – he is said to have grasped the *Dao De Jing* at the age of seven – refused all worldly honours and riches and went west into the mysterious mountain world of Sichuan, which is to this day considered to be the place of origin of all miracles and secret teachings in China. There, after a period of fasting and meditation, he met Lao Zi himself in a supernatural manner and the latter handed him a magical secret scroll. Later on he returned to the Dragon and Tiger Mountain (Lung Hu Shan) in the province of Jiangxi, where he attained immortality. His disciples and descendants were later given land by the rulers of the Wei, the Tang and Song dynasties, and even the Mongols were generous. The title of Tian Shi, or 'Master from Heaven', was hereditary in his family; rather like the title of the Tibetan Dalai Lama, the same personality was reincarnated in a child of the family whenever the current Master from Heaven died, the incarnation being revealed in a supernatural manner. The office of the Master from Heaven has sometimes been called that of a Daoist pope. This is not quite justified, because although the Master from Heaven has absolute power over daemons and ghosts, who are subject to his magic spells and unable to resist, he only has moral influence, without any constitutional foundation, upon the Daoist 'church' – if, in fact, one may speak of such a thing.

We can follow the development of Daoism thus far. Later, under the influence of advancing Buddhism, it was to develop into something quite different from what it was originally meant to be. An account of these changes, however, does not belong within the framework of a review of Daoism after Lao Zi, but in a general history of Chinese religion.

NOTES ON THE TEXT

PART I: DAO

Section 1

This section represents, in a sense, the theoretical foundation of the whole work. It begins with a demarcation against the common purely practical application of the concepts of DAO, and 'name'. In the declining years of the Zhou dynasty, the term DAO, or 'way' (see Introduction to this edition) had often been understood as the sum total of the teachings about leading the people that had been handed down from the ancient kings. This limited historical application of DAO is not what Lao Zi has in mind. His concept (or 'name') is supra-temporal, and therefore does not apply to anything that empirically exists. Thus Lao Zi departs from historical tradition and turns to speculation.

There he finds being in its dual form: as being-in-and-of-itself, and as existence. In the negative form of absolute being lies the potentiality of the existence of the world, i.e. of the spiritual (Heaven) and the material (Earth); while in existence the continuous rebirth of individual beings takes place. Cognition works in the same way: the path towards the absolute leads to cognition of the transcendent (thinking); the path towards existence leads to cognition of the world of spatial extent and individuation. These two ('thinking' and 'being', as Spinoza would say) are, however, only properties of the all-One, identical in essence and different only in appearance. The symbolic figure of the *tai ji* (the primal beginning) may be used to explain this unity.

This figure played a major part in ancient Chinese thought. It has been used since in endless playful representations – the 'being-within-each-other' of the positive and the negative, for example, where the white half of the circle which contains a black circle with a white dot represents the positive, male, light principle, and the correspondingly constructed black half of the circle symbolises the negative, female, dark principle. This is probably what is meant by the 'great secret of the unity of existence and non-existence' (the μη ὄν, wherever Lao Zi speaks of 'non-existence'). The still deeper secret of the secret would then be what is called *wu ji* (the 'non-beginning', which is even beyond *tai ji*) in which all differences are as yet unseparated and intermingled with one another. This is represented by a simple circle:

This is, in a sense, the mere potentiality of existence, or chaos. See section 25.

For the 'gateway of DAO' cf. Confucius, *Analects*, book VI, 15.

Section 2

Here cognition of good and evil is depicted as the beginning of evil, rather as in Genesis 3. Lao Zi adds the generalisation that within the phenomenal world the positing of the one necessarily posits its opposite, since all opposites occasion and condition one another. Lao Zi's demand for a 'beyond good and evil' is thus essentially different from Nietzsche's.

Of particular interest is the remark that 'good' is the summit of the beautiful, not something qualitatively different from it. This is quite in line with the terminology used throughout the work. 'Good' can also be translated as 'competent'. It is none other than the ideal of truth and beauty translated into action. In this respect, the work of the ancient Chinese thinker joins hands with the most modern treatises on the highest ideas.

The often-repeated phrase 'Thus also is the Man of Calling' usually introduces the practical application of a theoretical exposition. The 'Man of Calling' is man-in-accord-with-DAO, the 'saint' or the 'prophet', who is also called upon to rule the world. According to some Chinese sources, all the passages in which this formula occurs are quotations from a lost work called *Fen Dian*.

The teaching on 'effectiveness without action' which runs through the whole work, is here put forward for the first time. The idea is analogous to Tolstoy's 'doing nothing'. It means allowing the creative forces to work within and through one's own ego, without wanting to supplement it by external means. It is true that this is an ideal found quite generally in Chinese philosophy; and Confucius also mentions it as the highest ideal (cf. *Analects*, book XV, 4). However, it is only the 'mystics' who use it consistently in this particular sense. To this extent, it belongs to all ages. Cf. Goethe's and Spinoza's views in this respect. (Ch. Schrempf, *Goethes Weltanschauung*, I, pp. 179 ff.)

Lines 5 to 10, which rhyme in the original, are probably a quotation from an older collection of sayings.

Section 3

Lines 8ff.: The heart is the seat of desire for extraneous, alien things. In the Chinese listing of the five senses, the heart stands for 'sense of touch', 'sensing'. If the heart is empty, man is not bound to the external world by the ties of longing.

The 'body' and 'bones' are figurative terms for the natural basis of human existence. Their needs must be satisfied; if they are not, desires may be aroused by dissatisfaction, which would then extend to other things.

Cognition, in the sense of extraneous knowledge, is also considered evil (cf. section 2).

Section 4

The word *di*, which Strauss translates as 'Lord' means, on the one hand, the divine ruler of most ancient antiquity, and on the other the hypostatised Lord of Heaven, the 'ancestor' and the highest god.

Four sentences which are repeated in section 56 have been omitted here.

For the very difficult passage 'I do not know whose son it is' – elsewhere rendered as 'whose man's son it is' – see section 25 below, where it reads 'I do not know its name'.

Section 5

'Goodness' or 'morality', the highest concept of Confucianism, is rejected as imperfect since it does not reach beyond personal interest.

Straw dogs were made and dressed in festive garments in preparation for sacrifice, but once they had served their purpose they were discarded. The message this conveys is that all individual beings are most perfectly equipped for the purpose of their species, and there can be no question of 'regard for the person'.

The space between Heaven and Earth as the place in which life is generated is an idea which relates to the biblical 'fortress' (Genesis 1). Cf. section 6. The translation 'flute' follows Liang Qu-Chao; elsewhere it has been translated as 'bellows'.

Section 6

According to Lie Zi this section derives from the *Book of the Yellow Emperor*.

The 'valley' is a term that occurs frequently in the text (cf. sections 28, 39 in particular). Its literal meaning is the *empty* space between the slopes of mountains, not what we usually think of when using the term. Figuratively, as it is used here and in section 39, its meaning may be rendered as 'matter', in the sense of the still unformed, invisible, sheer potentiality of existence. 'Spirit' is then the active, form-giving principle. The Second Commentary remarks on this: 'It is called "valley" because it still has no existence; it is called "spirit" because it is nonetheless not "not" '. One could almost translate this as 'Spirit and matter in their unity are eternal'.

In relation to this passage, one should also consider that spirits (*shen*) in ancient China were frequently located near mountains (cf. Shan Hai Jing). The ancient custom of burying sacrificial gifts points to a chthonic cult. The investigations of Chavannes (*Le Dieu du sol dans l'ancienne religion chinoise*) should be consulted in this context. According to him, the union of the deities of the soil and of the harvest

(*Dsi*) formed the deity of the Earth (*Di*), which was thought to be female; and this took place in the seventh century BC. In the present context the origin of this concept still shines through quite distinctly. However, the fact that the concept is philosophically elaborated here does seem to point to a considerable distance in time from those original ideas. Cf. in this respect, Confucius's agitation concerning certain customs in the service of chthonic gods (*Analects*, book III, 21).

The 'gateway of the dark female' is to be understood as similar to line 6 of section 1.

'Uninterrupted as though persistent': Heraclitus's view that everything is in a state of flux (πάντα ῥεῖ *panta rei*) may be helpful in understanding this line. A remark by Confucius, too, points in a similar direction (*Analects*, book IX, 16).

Section 8

The term 'water' is often used in the *Dao De Jing* as an image of DAO whose power dwells in staying below.

Concerning line 6 cf. Confucius, *Analects*, book IV, 1. This and the next five lines are presumably a quotation from an existing collection of wise sayings. The last two lines, however, belong again within the immediate context.

Line 12 may refer to the use of subjects for public works, with reference to the appointed time; a principle to be found throughout Chinese antiquity.

Section 9

Line 1: the image of a bowl of water which one must not fill to overflowing.

The second image refers to the edge of a knife. The meaning is the same as the proverb 'What is too sharp (acute) will become jagged'.

In the last line of this section some editors add 'When the work is done and glory follows', but this does not agree with the general approach of the work, and also breaks the rhythm. It is likely that a corruption of section 17 – 'When the work is done things take their course' (literally 'follow their course') – has found its way into this section.

Section 10

The first two lines, in their present form, do not really make sense. One probably has to accept that the text is corrupt here. The general idea is likely to be: 'Unity of striving provides undivided life, which is then capable of resisting death'. Cf. sections 22 and 39 on the effect of unity.

Line 12: the word I have translated as 'female bird' originally meant the female of any bird. It is very likely that this refers to an obscure creation myth. Compare the concept of the Holy Spirit as a dove in Christian iconography, and the image of the spirit brooding over the deep in Genesis 1. Later commentators understand the gates of Heaven as the orifices of the body.

Lines 12 and 13: the opposition between inner intuition and discursive knowledge that can be found throughout the teachings of Lao Zi. The Confucian school of thought openly disagreed with him on this, although Confucius also considered innate intuitive knowledge to be the highest. Cf. *Analects*, book XVI, 9.

The last four lines of this section are repeated in section 51: again, this is probably traditional wisdom.

Section 12

The five colours are: blue (or green), red, yellow, white and black. The five tones (in English notation) are C, D, E, G, A. The five flavours, literally the 'five kinds of taste', are: bitter, salt, sweet, sour, sharp. The passage emphasises the importance of caring for one's inner independence, and the need to avoid yielding to cravings for the external things of the world of the senses. See also section 3.

Section 13

The text of this section is in rather poor condition. It would appear that part of an older commentary found its way into it after line 2 (lines 3-

11). I have applied the meaning of the rest of the passage to the translation of the first two lines.

The final sentence is repeated twice.

Section 14

The three names of DAO, 'seed', 'subtle' and 'small' designate its transcendence. Any attempts to read from the Chinese sounds *yi*, *he*, *wei* the name of the Hebrew God may safely be considered as rejected for good. (Victor von Strauss still believed in it: cf. his own translation.)

We do not deny that there are parallels between this view of DAO, i.e. as godhead, and the Israelite view. But such coincidences are understandable enough without any direct contact between the two cultures. This view of the godhead simply implies that human consciousness has reached a certain level in its cognition of the divine. In addition, the fundamental difference between the impersonal, pantheist concept of Lao Zi and the sharply outlined historical personality of the Israelite God should not be ignored.

The closing lines of this section refer to the supra-historicity of this truth: in this truth, past and present are one. Historicity, which plays such an important part in the thought of Confucius, necessarily fades into meaninglessness for Lao Zi. Although he frequently uses ancient notions of truth (cf. the multiple quotations) he does so only insofar as they coincide with his own approach. He stands beside them, but does not base himself upon them (cf. section 15).

Section 15

It is possible that the closing lines of section 14 should be more closely linked with the opening lines of this section. The description of the old 'Masters of Mysteries' may be applied to Lao Zi himself, as well as to mystics in general. It is of the essence of the mystic that he is hidden from the outside world, since he is no longer capable of taking outward life as something essentially serious; for this reason he is difficult to understand. We know something of the ironical, and often brutally sarcastic ways of such mystics from reading about the life of Confucius (*Analects*, book XVIII, 5, 6, 7, 8). Confucius felt particularly defenceless when faced with such people.

The translation of the last ten lines is given according to the Second

Commentary, which presents less difficulties than other variants. According to Wang Bi's edition one would have to translate: 'Who can make muddy water clear by making it still? Who can create stillness by moving it for a long time?'

The closing lines again show a connection with the thought of the section which follows. The final line is translated in accordance with the commentary of Wang Fu Zhi, who separates the group of phrases 'Remaining small, not becoming renewed, completing'. Others connect them as: 'He can remain small and escape new becoming'. It is not to be assumed that 'new becoming' indicates the idea of metempsychosis; it simply seems to suggest 'withdrawal into seclusion'.

Section 16

Lines 11ff. somehow interrupt the approach to the ascending scale at the end of the section. They are probably interpolated from somewhere else in order to justify the use of the term 'cognition' which is not commonly used in the text (cf. section 3), or to replace it with the word 'clarity'.

Line 10 occurs again in section 55, in better context.

The closing phrase which appears a bit lame here, also occurs in section 52.

On the ascending scale itself, the Second Commentary remarks: 'Cognition of eternity makes the heart empty, so that space becomes available to receive beings' (cf. section 49). If one thus 'receives beings' into oneself, partisan inclinations and disinclinations disappear. At the highest level this being is Heaven, which has both its prefiguration and goal in DAO. See also section 25.

Section 17

This hierarchy or ranking of princes is characteristic. Two lines following line 5, which also occur in section 23, have here been omitted.

In connection with the last three lines in this section one may draw comparisons with a rather appealing folk song which was sung in the time of the Emperor Yao.

> The sun rises and I go to work.
> The sun sets and I go to rest.
> I dig a well and I drink.
> I plough a field and I eat.
> The emperor: What does he give me?

(That is, all this I owe not to the emperor but to my own work.)

Section 18

These paradoxes illustrate the theoretical sentence in lines 1ff. of section 2, and the second half of section 38. The meaning of this section is that as long as everything is well ordered, the virtues mentioned are so common and natural they they do not catch the eye. A nice illustration of this can be found in a short fable: a long time ago, a Chinese man gave a Japanese man a book of the famous twenty-four examples of filial piety. The Japanese is said to have expressed great surprise that piety was considered something so extraordinary that one could find only twenty-four examples of it in all history. In Japan, however, piety was such an ordinary thing that nobody ever talked about it and one could find at the most twenty-four examples of lack of piety.

Line 5: 'relatives' refer literally to the six grades of relations: father, mother, older brother, younger brother, wife and children.

Section 19

If one returns to Nature and turns away from the way of culture, then all relationships will fall into place. Here again we find a contrast with the line of thought whose main representative was Confucius. Later Confucians, Han Yu in particular, have specifically used these paradoxical pronouncements to wage a passionate battle against Lao Zi, denouncing him as an obscurantist.

The first line of the next section has been added to this one.

Section 20

This section is often misunderstood because the relationship between the first two lines and the second two lines is overlooked, and they are then translated as: 'Between "definitely" and "probably" (i.e. between the definite, masculine, and the reluctant, feminine forms of affirmation) there is no essential difference. How great, by contrast, is the difference between good and evil!' My point of view is affirmed by section 2.

One bars one's way to an understanding of the tragic complaints of the lonely individualist amidst the 'unbroken' life-enjoying world of Men which follow, if one takes the bitter irony of lines 3 and 4 as a flat and shallow exhortation. The complaint about loneliness, coming as it does from the man who is 'the sole sensitive heart among ghastly masks', is of great interest in the context of the history of religion, as it is the reverse side of religious individualism. Here we are faced with a typical phenomenon that is always and necessarily linked with the attainment of a higher level of development. It is particularly interesting because of the fact that in China the social psyche has won a victory over the individual psyche.

Line 6: 'Oh loneliness, how long will you last?' In this we follow the prevailing tradition. Others have translated: 'The sage's cognition is unlimited and immeasurable.'

Line 10: 'Only I am so reluctant, I have not yet been given a sign'. The 'sign' came from the oracle which had to be consulted (in antiquity tortoise-shells were set alight and the answers read from the cracks that appeared in them). This sign had to be given before anything could be undertaken. In the present context it probably needs to be understood in a broader sense. Cf. Confucius's complaint that he had received no sign (*Analects*, book IX, 8).

Line 20: 'Unquiet, alas, like the sea'. Here we follow Wang Bi's version. Other translations have 'unquiet as if obscured'.

Section 21

In this section the descending line from the Life (here called 'the great') to reality is drawn, corresponding to the ascending line in section 16. See also section 15.

From DAO life emerges. The emergence of existence passes through the stages of 'ideas', (spiritual) 'being', 'seed' and 'reality'.

Lines 11-13: This final paragraph has also been translated differently in the Second Commentary: 'From ancient times to this day one cannot make do without its name, since from it all beginnings emerge'. The emergence of all things from DAO makes it possible to understand them by virtue of DAO; that is, because existence has an immanent logic it can be logically perceived.
(The final comment also occurs in section 54.)

Section 22

In the first six lines there is another quotation from a rhyming adage; at the end of the section this is expressly identified as a pronouncement by the ancients. (Cf. section 77.)

Line 1: the image of the moon, at first incomplete and then becoming complete; line 2: the image of a caterpillar or a rope, indicating the change from a state of tension to one of relaxation. Line 3 is interpreted as a hollow in the ground that becomes filled with water (cf. Mencius, IV, B, 18). Line 4: the image of the self-renewing leaves of a tree. All of these are the positive expressions of what is negatively expressed in section 24.

The lines 'He encompasses the One and sets an example to the world' are also found in section 39.

Section 23

The second half of this section presents great difficulties. The text varies significantly in different editions, and this adds to the suspicion that it has been corrupted.

There are marked differences among existing editions in the interpretation of the word that I have rendered here as 'poverty' – literally, it means 'to lose'. No less difficult is the term I have translated as 'coming to meet joyfully', and which literally means 'to be happy to receive'. Both the Second Commentary and St Julien leave out the 'to be happy', and thus make the text flow more easily; but it is doubtful whether this is not a belated alleviation. Wang Bi understands 'loss' in the sense that I do here. He says: 'The Man of Calling can bear everything and identify with everything'; and therefore also with 'losing', or 'poverty'. Others – Strauss for instance – understand 'loss' as 'corruption'. In that case one comes to an impossible conclusion: 'Whoever attains unity of being through following DAO will be joyfully received and assimilated by DAO. DAO moves towards him, furthers and completes his striving and rejoices in keeping him safe.' A similar difficulty occurs with 'virtue' (in other words, the term that I have translated as Life) which, like 'corruption', is either rhetorically personified here, or else considered as represented by those who have already identified with it: 'Corruption, however, enjoys corrupting him who unites himself to it.' (Strauss, loc. cit., p. 123.) This is based, in fact, on yet another text. I would suggest that such personifications contradict Lao Zi's wholly pantheistic approach and in the second and third part also contradict Chinese linguistic instinct. On the other hand we have Carus's interpretation (loc. cit., p. 109): 'When a man is identified with reason he forsooth joyfully embraces reason, when identified with virtue he forsooth joyfully embraces virtue, and when identified with loss he forsooth joyfully embraces loss.' This interpretation, too, is grammatically impossible.

St Julien translates 'Celui qui s'identifie au Tao gagne le Tao etc'. The Second Commentary considers the passage an expression of a sentence of retribution, according to which everyone receives what his deeds are worth or deserve. On the whole, it is probably sensible to give up the passage as hopelessly beyond interpretation.

The last line can also be found in connection with section 17.

Section 24

Cf. section 22. The term 'festering sore' has also been translated as 'annoying behaviour'. The meaning would then appear to be: 'Whoever tries to stand out spoils the merit he has in the eyes of the world (i.e. of 'created beings', gods and men) by his arrogance, and this way makes himself an annoyance.' Compare the New Testament, 'They have their reward . . . etc.'.

Section 25

The term I have translated as 'man' really means 'king'. What is meant is the highest ruler on earth, the representative of mankind and guardian of moral order on earth. As he uses the word so often, Lao Zi has therefore turned to the term 'man'. The fourth which is added here to the usual triad of Heaven, Earth and man, and which comprises them all, is DAO. For the ascending scale in the last four lines, cf. section 16.

Section 26

When one travels in China one always has to carry a 'heavy load', as there are few domestic comforts at the hostel. Many a European travelling in China has found this to be true – much to his distress – when he arrives at night at an empty hostel, while his bedlinen etc. is still miles behind him. The image is therefore quite realistic.

A different version of the last line but one exists: 'By lightheartedness one loses the ministers. By restlessness one loses the ruler.' My translation is, however, borne out by the opening lines of the section.

Section 27

This section also begins with a sequence of rhyming adages. According to the publisher of Wang Bi's commentary the first four lines, which are nowadays included in all editions, appear only in He Shang Gong's version and are said to have been omitted in earlier editions.

For the passages about good men as teachers of the non-good, and the non-good as material (in the sense of 'pupil material') for the good, cf. Confucius, *Analects*, book II, 20.

The high esteem for one's teachers, and their love for their pupils ('pupil material') has been interpreted by some as reciprocal duty. This, does not, however, make good sense. It is better to assume that the Man of Calling loves all his people, those whom he has appointed as teachers, as well as those whom he has given to the teachers as 'material' for instruction. The final remarks only make sense in this context.

Section 28

This section consists of three symmetrically structured strophes, complete in themselves. The mention of simplicity at the end has caused some editors to add a few aphorisms on simplicity which do not in fact belong in this context. They might be fragments taken from section 37.

The 'uncreated' (*wu ji*) in the second stanza is the state before the primal beginning (*tai ji*) in which all opposites are intermingled. For the 'valley of the world' see the note to section 6.

Section 29

The 'world', literally 'that which is under Heaven', is equivalent to the Roman *orbis terrarum*, and also the 'realm'. 'Spiritual thing' (*shen qi*) is an old expression, and literally means 'spiritual or divine implement'. The expression probably derives from the nine legendary sacrificial vessels which were made by the great Yu and were handed on from generation to generation as a symbol of lordship over what was then the nine provinces. The phrase is used figuratively here: it means that the realm is a spiritual organism which cannot be dealt with by contrived, soulless or mechanical action.

The rhyming adages in this section strangely resemble Goethe's 'Coptic Song', II – although the moral drawn from them here is diametrically opposed to the one drawn there.

Section 30

Line 1: 'Ruler of men' is another expression for 'prince'. Line 3 can be rendered: 'For such things easily fall back' (i.e. upon their author).

Lines 4 and 5 speak of the effect of war on men, lines 6 and 7 of the effect of war on *mana*, i.e. the forces of nature that are disturbed by it. The meaning of what follows is that war should be considered only as a necessary evil, without any purpose in itself.

Three lines at the end of the section have been omitted here: they were taken from section 55, but are more relevant to that section.

Section 31

This section probably provides a commentary on the preceding one, and it seems to have been added at a later date. Wang Bi passes it over without mention. Apparently it is not to be found in any of the old manuscripts. Cf. Epigraph on Wang Bi.

Section 32

Lines 2–9: the passage from 'Even though it is small' to 'would find their balance . . .' interrupts the context and is probably taken from section 37, like the final lines of section 28.

This section, which in some respects resembles section 1, gives Lao Zi's view on the question of clarifying or rectifying concepts and conceptual terminology, apparently a much discussed topic in ancient times. Cf. Confucius's comment on the subject in *Analects*, book XIII, 3 and O. Franke, *Über die chinesische Lehre von den Bezeichnungen*, Leiden, 1906.

Section 33

A series of antitheses, in which the second term always represents the higher order. For this reason the third pair of lines, which in the original text reads 'Whoever is self-sufficient is rich. Whoever asserts himself (acts by force) has will-power' – needs to be rearranged in order to catch Lao Zi's meaning.

The final world 'lives' (in Chinese, *shou*) is used here in the sense of 'has eternal life'.

Section 34

This is about the omnipresence of DAO. There is some overlap with section 2. Some uncertainties occur in the text: instead of 'It clothes and nourishes all things' some editions have 'It loves and nourishes'.

Section 35

This section also starts with four rhyming adages. The 'great primal image' is the same as DAO. Cf. also section 14.

Section 36

Here we have a series of paradoxical sayings whose practical application shows a Machiavellian boldness.

The last two lines in this section are probably a hint at esoteric wisdom. I have therefore translated the term *li qi* as 'means of furthering' and not as some commentators do, as 'sharp weapons'. On this term, compare section 57, line 9, where it is translated as 'sharp implements'.

Section 37

The additional lines in sections 28 and 32 probably belong here. However I have dispensed with any attempt at reconstruction.

PART II: DE, or Life

Section 38

The range of actions here presents some difficulties because the same point ('acting and having designs') occurs twice: in relation to those who do not cherish Life and those who cherish justice. These difficulties can best be overcome by interpreting the 'non-cherishing of Life' as embracing 'love' ('morality'), 'justice' and 'custom' ('rites'). 'Acting and having designs' would then be the average of these three, amongst which love ranks a degree higher while morality hardly measures up at all. Love acts and has no designs, i.e. it is not self-seeking. The other levels are graded accordingly.

The presentation of 'moral' behaviour is rather drastic, for it is shown as capable of being unbearably oppressive with its 'rules of conduct'.

The passage which follows, 'If DAO is lost then Life . . . etc.', is as ambiguous in the original as it is in translation. Lao Zi may mean 'If DAO is lost then there will be Life . . . etc.', analogous to section 18. But this interpretation makes no satisfactory sense in relation to the first part of this section. Therefore the indications are that we should interpret it as: 'If DAO is lost then Life is lost together with it etc.'.

All this is in sharp contrast to Confucianism, whose highest values – love, justice, morality (propriety) – are here rejected. Although faith, the fourth of the cardinal values of Confucianism, is acknowledged, it is declared to be incommensurable with propriety; and the fifth, pre-knowledge, is described as the illusion of DAO.

'The right man': although a different term is used, this is nevertheless objectively identical with the 'Man of Calling'.

The last line of this section is repeated in a number of places.

Section 39

The One is identical with DAO.

The juxtaposition of the gods and the valley is reminiscent of section 6.

The passage about 'all things' is left out in some editions.

With regard to the pronouncement on kings and princes cf. section 22.

The term here translated as 'example' has been variously interpreted in other editions. Some have 'purity, chastity' instead. Other editions repeat the term 'example' instead of 'if kings and princes were not exalted by it'.

'Lonely', 'orphaned', 'trifling': this is how rulers would officially describe themselves in relation to Heaven. The relevant passage is repeated in section 42, and can therefore be omitted here.

The image of the carriage (a passage which is also rather doubtful and considered even by the Second Commentary as a corruption of the text) should probably be interpreted to mean that just as the carriage cannot exist without its individual parts, so the prince cannot exist without subjects. The opposite interpretation, according to which the concept of 'carriage' expresses more than its component parts reminds one strongly of Buddhist views, which deny *Atman* to the individual human being.

Section 40

'Return' signifies a cyclical movement, hence DAO is complete in itself and inexhaustible. 'Weakness' is a qualitative – not quantitative – effect. In this context, 'non-existence' is again that which does not enter into appearance, i.e. qualitative value. The principle that serves to explain here is teleology, not causality.

Section 41

The first half of this section presents no difficulties. In contrast, the quotation from 'the poet' contains stark paradoxes. Within this quotation, the meaning of DAO comes closer to that of 'way' than it does elsewhere.

The discrepancy between essence and appearance which is expressed in these lines comes about because all virtues in their highest form (of development) do nothing to put themselves into the limelight. Cf. 'Let not your right hand know what your left hand does' (in other words, do not let essence be ruled by appearance). The great quadrant has no corners because it is of infinite size and therefore eludes perception. A similar thought underlies the line on the 'great tone' – that is, that it exceeds the range of what is audible.

Section 42

This section comprises two separate parts. The first concerns the origins of the universe. The One or unity is *wu ji*, the Two or duality *tai ji* with its partition into *yang* and *yin*. See the note on section 1.

The Three, the 'flowing power' is the unifying medium of the two dualist powers.

The second part is to some extent a repetition of section 39.

The last line has also been translated as 'I want to be called father (or founder), of this teaching'. The present translation, however, is better documented in the commentaries.

Section 43

The 'softest thing' is that which does not resist.

Here, 'non-existence' must again be interpreted as the non-spatial, which is capable of pervading the spatial everywhere.

Section 45

The rhymed adages are similar to those in the second part of section 41.

Section 46

'When DAO rules on earth': Here DAO is not to be understood in its strict sense, but means rather: 'If rational conditions prevail'.

Section 47

Another interpretation of 'He does not need to see and yet is he clear' is '. . . and yet is he capable of giving orders'.

Section 48

For the last two sentences, see also section 57. The expression I have translated as 'realm' in this section is there rendered as 'world', in order to avoid a clash with the first line where another term is used for 'realm'; objectively, however, the meaning is the same.

Section 49

This section, too, expresses sentiments that are rather different from those of Confucianism. It is true that Confucius goes so far as to describe one's own demands or desires as the measure of one's treatment of the demands of others. Lao Zi, however, goes a step further by positing the ideal of treating everyone according to his essence, in other words as a pure purpose in himself. This is the meaning of the first two lines. 'The Man of Calling has no heart of his own', literally means 'no heart with a once-and-for-all determined direction of acting'. It is clear from the last two lines, in which Lao Zi implies that all people stare with surprise at such an exceptional phenomenon, that he is aware that he is expressing a paradox.

Of particular interest is the reason given for absolute goodness and faithfulness – that is, that they are founded in one's own essence (Life), which cannot help expressing itself in accordance with itself, regardless of how others behave.

Section 50

'Going out', i.e. from non-existence into existence, 'going in', i.e. from existence into non-existence. 'Companions of Life' are those in the ascending line, 'companions of death' those in the descending line.

'Men who live and thereby move towards the place of death' are those who, in their striving after life, seek 'that which lingers on' (cf. Goethe's 'Were I to say to the moment: O linger on . . .'); and by this yearning, make themselves vulnerable to death.

All of these add up to nine-tenths of men: given over to death. The remaining tenth are those who know 'how to live life well': these are the sages. Since all dangers only affect the individual ego, they are exempt and need not fear: for by abandoning their individual, accidental ego they have also abandoned their 'mortal spot'.

There is a school of thought that interprets this passage differently, translating 'thirteen' instead of 'three out of ten'. According to the latter there are thirteen powers of death and thirteen mortal points. However, this interpretation rests on rather shaky grounds, not only given the context of the passage, but also because no-one really knows what to make of the mysterious 'three multiplied by thirteen'. It is easy to see that later Daoist playfulness was well served by this interpretation. In subsequent readings of this passage, the search for a panacea for the tiger's claws and wounds caused by weapons has played its part. The Boxer Uprising with its blessing of arms, is the last relic of this superstition. That all this has nothing to do with Lao Zi needs no emphasis.

Section 51

The first two lines refer to the state before 'things' appear; the next two to the state after they have appeared – they are the consequences of the first two statements. Once things have found the ground of their existence in DAO and the power for their existence in Life, they create an external form for themselves through their own essence; then the surrounding circumstances give this form its final shape without there being any need for special intervention. This pattern in Nature is also the reason it is the highest wisdom for a ruler to refrain from all 'doing'.

Section 54

The sequence of social levels – person, family, community, country, world – is largely the same as that mentioned in the Confucian *Great Learning*: person, family, country, world. Lao Zi's use of a different word for 'country' can be attributed to editorial amendments by the Chinese commentators. It is of some interest that Lao Zi mentions the rural community.

For the last line cf. section 21.

Section 55

For an explanation of the victory over all dangers see section 50. A parallel can be found in the promises given by Christ in the apocryphal passage in Mark 16: 17ff. The passage 'It does not yet know about man and women and yet its blood stirs . . . etc.' is rendered by Strauss word for word in Greek.

'Abundance of peace' means inner harmony. Towards the end of this passage it is interesting to note the almost imperceptible antithesis between lines 14–15: 'To know peace means to be eternal. To know eternity means to be clear'; and lines 16–17: 'To increase life is called happiness' (cf. section 50), 'To apply one's strength one's desire' (we would say 'one's nervous energy') 'is called strong'. This antithesis is highlighted by the condemnation pronounced at the end.

The last lines are more appropriate to this section than to section 30.

Section 56

The first antithetical saying probably belongs in the context of section 81. The second saying is taken from section 52, and the following five from section 4. They are all more appropriate in those places than they are in this section, which describes the aloofness from all joys and sufferings of the world that is an attribute of the man who has recognised the truth.

The 'gates' are the sense organs which permit the outer world to enter, just as the mouth is the organ that permits the inner world to emerge. The mouth is here called *dui*. Cf. *Yi Jing*, hexagram 58.

Section 57

The term 'art of government' is a conjectural substitute for the term 'straightness' which is used in most translations. However, in the ancient Chinese language the two terms are sometimes interchangeable. My interpretation here is also borne out by the Japanese commentary.

There is yet another paradoxical antithesis between the first two sentences and the third.

The negative practical expositions largely agree with Confucius's pronouncements in *Analects*, book II, 1 and 3 – except that Confucius takes morality (propriety) as an important factor besides Life (power of the spirit), while Lao Zi accords morality a very low status (cf. section 38).

The section ends with the quotation of an ancient rhyming adage, instead of the usual, practical application of a theoretical statement.

Section 58

The meaning of the first four lines is quite clear. There are variations in the text in the rest of the section. My interpretation tries to convey the following meaning: 'What at first appears as misfortune (i.e. a reluctant handling of government) proves itself in time to be good fortune. What at first appears as an advantage (i.e. an energetically acting government which leads the people to glory and honour) brings misfortune as time goes by. Therefore the highest achievement is not to govern, for otherwise laws will, in time, become a burden (cf. Goethe's 'Reason becomes nonsense, good deeds a plague', *Faust*, Part I). And the people remain blinded.'

Another version of the text separates the two stanzas after line 6, thus adding this line to the preceding ones; this reads: 'But who recognises that good fortune and misfortune each at their zenith, continually flow into each other?' It continues: 'If the ruler is not of the right kind, order and goodness perpetually turn into their opposites and the people remain blinded (ignorant).'

One must assume that this is a textual corruption, and as a result one can make out its general meaning but not a specific line of thought.

This section and the preceding one go closely together in subject matter.

Section 60

In the passage concerning ghosts and their effects, the text presents some difficulties. In particular, it is unclear whether this refers only to the spirits of the dead or to nature spirits also. A possible translation – though just as difficult grammatically – would be: 'If one rules the world according to DAO then *mana* does not manifest itself as daemons (or nature spirits; in other words, they remain quiet). Apart from the fact that *mana* does not manifest itself in daemons, the daemons do not harm men' – i.e. they act 'normally', there will be no natural disasters: cf. section 20. Or: 'Apart from the fact that the daemons do not harm men the Man of Calling does not harm men either' (textual variant). 'If these two do not fight each other their powers are joined in beneficial effect.'

It is the word *fei* that causes the greatest difficulties. I have translated it in the text as 'not that' or 'not only', and rendered it above as 'apart from the fact that'. Simply to omit it, as St Julien does, is not permissible, because it occurs in all editions. All this notwithstanding, the meaning is in general clear: '*Quieta non movere*'! A 'reluctant' and peaceable government will have the effect that the invisible world will also remain calm; while in times of unrest 'signs and wonders' will occur.

Section 61

To 'keep oneself downstream' means to keep oneself free of pretence, to hold back.

The relationship between the great and the small realm that profits from mutual restraint consists in this: the greater realm by its restraint motivates the small one to affiliate itself (there are many examples of this in Chinese history); the small realm profits from the affiliation in terms of political influence, and is also assured of protection against enemy aggression. Generally speaking, this is the teaching according to which the state that serves the common weal in the most disinterested way attains hegemony.

Section 62

The word *ao*, here translated as 'homeland', really means the dark, south-western corner of the house where the household gods (the Roman *lares*) have their domicile. The worship of the *lares* seems to have already receded in the sixth century BC in favour of the gods of the hearth who have won outright by this time. Concerning these conditions cf. Confucius, *Analects*, book III, 13.

By applying the ways of this deity, who dwells in the dark recesses and from there protects the house, to DAO in a broad sense, Lao Zi achieves a remarkable image which is further explained in the lines 2–3. Of particular interest is the extension of its effectiveness even to the non-good. Cf. Schiller's 'Ode to Joy':

> All the Good and all the Evil
> follow (in) its trail of roses.

The two lines on beautiful words and honourable conduct have been rendered according to the text of *Huai-Nan-Zi*. The passage presents a great deal of textual difficulty.

I have followed the Second Commentary concerning the institution of the ruler and the princes as it relates to the above, i.e. they are to take care that even the non-good should not be rejected. The lines that follow are based on the image of offerings made to the ruler, and describe DAO as the most valuable gift. Another possible translation would be: 'Better than a minister who (knowing the whole ceremonial in the presence of the ruler) reverently holds his bejewelled sceptre in his hands, and draws up in procession with four horsemen in front of him, is the man who offers DAO kneeling (literally, 'sitting'), according to the ancient rite.' The details of the court ceremonial which are hinted at here do not warrant a lengthy explanation, since they are not essential to the context.

The idea of forgiveness of sins which occurs here is generally alien to Confucianism in such religious terms.

Section 63

The phrase 'repays animosity with Life', which is usually translated as 'repays injustice with goodness', plays a certain part in the discourses of the time. Lao Zi justifies it in section 49 by saying that our mode of action emanates from our essence, and therefore we cannot but be good. He thus goes beyond the idea of 'mutuality' that occupies such a prominent position in post-Confucian systems. Confucius had doubts about this as far as public justice was concerned (cf. his pronouncement in this respect in *Analects*, book XIV, 36), although he acknowledges the principle as valid for private (individual) morality (cf. *Li Ji*, 19, 11ff).

Section 64

Paying attention to what is small, to what has not yet entered into appearance is a principle that Confucius acknowledges too (cf. *Analects*, book XV, ii). Apart from this it looks like a quotation from the *Book of Records*. Cf. *Shu Jing*, IV, 5, 8, 9: 'Do not do anything worthless that would damage what is valuable – thus your work shall attain completion. Do not cherish strange things while neglecting those that are useful – thus will the people have plenty. Do not keep dogs and horses that are not suited to the climate. Do not feed precious birds and rare animals in the country. Do not cherish things from far countries – thus the people will come from afar. You shall cherish only those who are worthy – thus the people who are near will have peace. Early or late: never be idle. Do not neglect trifling actions, for in the end these influence the great power of being, just like a mountain nine fathoms high that lacks the last bucketful of earth.' (Cf. Confucius's point of view on this issue, in *Analects*, book IX, 18.)

Section 65

With regard to educating the people, Lao Zi and Confucius are quite in agreement (cf. *Analects*, book VIII, 9).

Section 66

This section as well as the apocryphal section 31 receives no comment from Wang Bi. The present commentator has nothing new to offer either.

NOTES ON THE TEXT

Section 67

The beginning of this section is not quite clear in the text, and has traditionally been considered so. Some editions leave out the word DAO without this resulting in any real change in meaning.

The interpretation: 'All the world says my teaching is absolutely useless', which some prefer, is significant. My own interpretation is borne out by the context.

Section 69

Objectively, this section belongs with sections 30 and 31. 'It is better to play the guest than to play the lord' implies that one should orientate one's movements towards those of the enemy. The paradoxical sayings are simply intended as strong expressions of the caution to be observed in war.

Line 11: The 'treasure' should be seen in conjunction with the preceding section. The line is actually dubious textually.

Line 13: Most commentaries change the word *ai* ('with a heavy heart'), to *rang* ('to retreat'). The translation would then read: 'The one who retreats will win victory'.

Section 70

Like Confucius, Lao Zi had to deal with the problem of not being understood. There is probably nothing more characteristic than the way in which each of the two deals with this fact. For Confucius the greatest source of pain was not to be understood, and he probably never quite managed to cope with it. The fact that he talks so much – from the opening sentence in the *Analects* – about the need to rise above being misunderstood or misjudged, is an indication of how deeply the problem affected him. We know that it was not wounded pride that caused this response, but the conviction that while he had the means to help the realm there was no one prepared to apply these means. Lao Zi, however, dismisses the problem in pride and sovereignty, secure in the knowledge that being misjudged or misunderstood results from the fact that DAO, the 'lord and ancestor' of his teaching and its underlying principle, is not perceived or recognised. He belongs to the catena of sages who have resigned themselves to this fact once and for all, whose like we meet many times in the *Analects* of Confucius, especially in book XVIII. For the mystic this attitude is quite natural. In this respect Lao Zi has 'kindred spirits' at all times, and in all nations.

Section 71

The pictogram I have translated as 'suffering' literally means 'to be ill'. The stark paradox in this section results from the fact that the term is used both as a noun and as a verb. A similar pronouncement on knowledge can be found in the *Analects* of Confucius, book II, 17, which is equally significant for its concurrence with and its deviation from the teachings of Lao Zi.

Section 72

The 'terrible' thing that people should fear is probably death: cf. section 74. A multitude of other interpretations of the passage exist.

Section 74

Various interpretations of this section exist. Some see it simply as a warning against the death penalty, or even as a recommendation to restrict political murder. Accordingly they translate lines 3ff. as follows (the words in brackets represent translators' insertions and are not in the original text): 'Keep people in constant fear of death, and if someone does something strange (i.e. evil) then I shall take him and kill him. Who dares (then still to do evil deeds)? But there is one (executioner? – according to others: a properly appointed judge) who has to pronounce the death penalty . . .'

The many insertions that are necessary prove how forced the interpretation is; quite apart from the fact that this view is far from Lao Zi's own line of thought. Conversely, it is easy to see that in China where nowadays [1910] the death penalty is commonplace, the commentators have adapted their interpretation of the text to vulgar public opinion. It is not made clear who has the power over life and death.

Section 76

The line 'When trees are strong they are cut down' is interpreted in different ways in various editions and does present difficulties: the text is probably corrupt here.

Section 77

The Chinese bow bends inwards when it is unstrung, and has to be pressed outwards when strung.

Unstrung Bow:

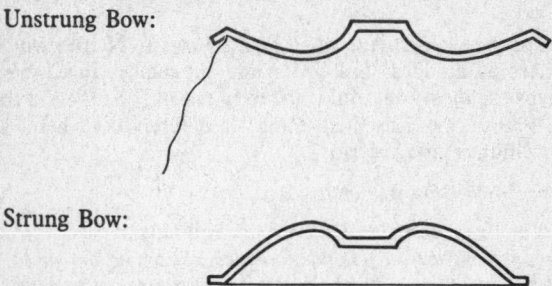

Strung Bow:

Cf. also section 22.

Section 78

Here again, the lines in this section are quoted from other sources.

The chthonic sacrifices (cf. note to section 6) are the privilege of the sovereign. The prince or the emperor is also the lord of the earth's sacrifice.

The assumption of guilt as a precondition for lordship is a common belief in Chinese antiquity as well as in western Asia and Europe. Cf. the prayers of Kings Tang and Wu, quoted in Confucius, *Analects*, book X, 1.

The closing line expressed in modern terms would read: 'Truth often sounds paradoxical'.

Section 79

The meaning is probably that after every quarrel, even if it is settled, there still remains a residue of discord. To avoid this one must avoid quarrelling altogether; this is achieved by acknowledging duties but without claiming rights for oneself. Cf. Confucius, *Analects*, book XV, 20.

Section 80

In ancient China – and in Peru – rope-knotting served as a substitute for writing (cf. also the Nordic runes).

The description of the Golden Age when man returns to Nature which Lao Zi announces as an ideal has had many resonances in Chinese literature. Perhaps the most beautiful is the fairy tale of 'The Well in the Peach Blossom Forest', by Tao Yuan-Ming. It is reproduced here, as rendered by Dr Gutherz of Qingdao:

The Well in the Peach-Blossom Forest

In the time of Tai Yuan, there lived a fisherman in Wuling. One day he travelled upstream along a river. He had forgotten whether he had gone near or far when a great forest, hundreds of yards deep, and aglow with peach blossoms, appeared on either side of the river. There were no other trees in the forest, only beautiful fresh, scented grass, into which the peach petals fell. The fisherman was amazed and travelled onward, for he wanted to know where the forest would end.

At the edge of the forest stood the mountain from which the river flowed. A narrow entrance led into the mountain itself, which looked as though it was surrounded by light. The fisherman walked into this entrance, following a straight path; but after a few steps it became light and wide, and a broad, spreading land lay before his eyes.

Neat huts and tidy houses stood among good fields and beautiful, shallow waters. Paths crossed one another; there were all kinds of bamboo, and many mulberry trees; chickens and dogs answered one another from village to village. Men and women sowed the fields – just as it is with us. Children and old folk were peaceful and serene in what they were doing.

The people were astonished when they saw our fisherman, and questioned him eagerly. As he talked, they gave him wine to drink and slaughtered chickens for a meal. The villagers heard about it all, and everyone gathered to ask him questions. They told their own tale of how, long ago in the turbulent times of Qin Shi Huang, their ancestors had left and come to this place – women, children and all the people. Since that time no one had ever gone back, and so they knew nothing of people outside. They asked who was king. They did not know the dynasty of Han, much less the Wei and the Jin. But the fisherman brought them tidings of all he knew, and they listened to him. He passed many a day in this manner, feasted and entertained with food and wine. When the time came for them to part, the villagers thought it would not be worthwhile to tell the people outside about it all.

Finally the fisherman left this land, returned to the river, and stepped into his boat. He remembered the place and its surroundings well. Back in the district capital, he reported to the official, who sent out messengers on the strength of the fisherman's report. However they lost their way . . .

It is true that later Liu Ji Qi, 'the Wise Man of the South', went boldly forth to search for the place. But before getting there he fell ill and died. Since then no one has asked the way.

BIBLIOGRAPHY

Nian Er Zi He Gu (Collected Works of the 22 Philosophers), Shanghai 1894, Lithograph. Volume 1: Lao Tse. Commentary by Wang Bi. Critique of the text by Lu De Ming. Cited as Wang Bi.

Lao Zi Ji Jie by Sui Hui (2 volumes). Woodprint dated 1528. Very thorough commentary, not only explaining the overall meaning of the *Dao De Jing* (as Wang Bi does) but providing a detailed grammatical exegesis. The interpretation of the text shows, in parts, some substantial differences from that of Wang Bi. Cited as Second Commentary.

Dao De Jing Che by Hong Ying-Shao (2 volumes). Woodprint, like the Second Commentary from the time of the Ming dynasty (1368-1644), undated.

Lao Zi De Jie by Dazai Shuntai (2 volumes). This is the work of a Japanese scholar from the school of Butsu Sorais. Dazai Shuntai was a keen advocate of original Confucian teaching. In his old age he changed his allegiance to Lao Zi. His work was completed posthumously (1747) and published by one of his disciples.

Wang Fu Zhi, Chinese scholar who lived during the late years of the Ming dynasty: the volume containing a commentary on Lao Zi has been consulted from among his collected works.

In addition to these texts a number of other Chinese works have been consulted peripherally. There does not seem to be any need to list them here. This applies, too, to a manuscript from the library of the Taiqinggong monastery in the Lao Shan mountains near Qingdao; careful perusal of this did not yield any essentially new information or interpretation.

BIBLIOGRAPHY

English Literature

James Legge, *The Sacred Books of the East*, Vol. XXXIX: The Texts of Taoism, Oxford 1891.

F.H. Balfour, *Taoist Texts*, London 1884.

Paul Carus, *Lao Tze's Tao-Teh-King*, Chicago 1898.

Lionel Giles, *The Sayings of Lao Tzu*, London 1905. Second edition 1909.

C. Spurgeon Medhurst, *The Tao Teh King*, Chicago 1905.

French Literature

C. De Harlez, *Textes taoistes* (Annales du Musée Guimet, Tome XX), Paris 1891.

Léon de Rosny, *Le Taoisme*, Paris 1892. (This is not a translation from the Chinese but a comprehensive compilation of existing texts on Daoism.)

Stanislas Julien, *Lao Tseu, Tao Te King. Le livre de la voie et de la vertue*, composé dans le VIe siècle avant l'ère chrétienne par le philosophe Lao Tseu, traduit en française et publié avec le texte chinois et un commentaire perpetuel. Paris 1842.

German Literature

Victor von Strauss, *Lao Tse's Tao Te King*, Leipzig 1870.

Franz Hartmann, *Theosophie in China*. Betrachtungen über das Tao-Teh-King. Aus dem Chinesischen (?) des Lao-Tse übersetzt. Leipzig, undated. (*RW doubts whether this is in fact a translation from a Chinese original. – Trans.*)

Joseph Kohler, Des Morgenlandes groesste Weisheit. Laotse, Tao-Te-King. Berlin and Leipzig 1908.

Julius Grill, Lao-Tses Buch vom hoechsten Wesen und vom höchsten Gut. Tübingen 1910.

[. . .]

PENGUIN

ARKANA

NEW AGE BOOKS FOR MIND, BODY & SPIRIT

With over 200 titles currently in print, Arkana is the leading name in quality books for mind, body and spirit. Arkana encompasses the spirituality of both East and West, ancient and new. A vast range of interests is covered, including Psychology and Transformation, Health, Science and Mysticism, Women's Spirituality, Zen, Western Traditions and Astrology.

If you would like a catalogue of Arkana books, please write to:

Sales Dept. – Arkana
Penguin Books USA Inc.
375 Hudson Street
New York, NY 10014

Arkana Marketing Department
Penguin Books Ltd
27 Wrights Lane
London W8 5TZ

ARKANA – NEW-AGE BOOKS FOR MIND, BODY AND SPIRIT

A selection of titles already published or in preparation

Neal's Yard Natural Remedies Susan Curtis, Romy Fraser and Irene Kohler

Natural remedies for common ailments from the pioneering Neal's Yard Apothecary Shop. An invaluable resource for everyone wishing to take responsibility for their own health, enabling you to make your own choice from homeopathy, aromatherapy and herbalism.

The Arkana Dictionary of New Perspectives Stuart Holroyd

Clear, comprehensive and compact, this iconoclastic reference guide brings together the orthodox and the highly unorthodox, doing full justice to *every* facet of contemporary thought – psychology and parapsychology, culture and counter-culture, science and so-called pseudo-science.

The Absent Father: Crisis and Creativity Alix Pirani

Freud used Oedipus to explain human nature; but Alix Pirani believes that the myth of Danae and Perseus has most to teach an age which offers 'new responsibilities for women and challenging questions for men' – a myth which can help us face the darker side of our personalities and break the patterns inherited from our parents.

Woman Awake: A Celebration of Women's Wisdom Christina Feldman

In this inspiring book, Christina Feldman suggests that it *is* possible to break out of those negative patterns instilled into us by our social conditioning as women: confirmity, passivity and surrender of self. Through a growing awareness of the dignity of all life and its connection with us, we can regain our sense of power and worth.

Water and Sexuality Michel Odent

Taking as his starting point his world-famous work on underwater childbirth at Pithiviers, Michel Odent considers the meaning and importance of water as a symbol: in the past – expressed through myths and legends – and today, from an advertisers' tool to a metaphor for aspects of the psyche. Dr Odent also boldly suggests that the human species may have had an aquatic past.

ARKANA – NEW-AGE BOOKS FOR MIND, BODY AND SPIRIT

A selection of titles already published or in preparation

Women Mystics of the Twentieth Century   Anne Bancroft

Throughout history women have sought answers to eternal questions about existence and beyond – yet most gurus, philosophers and religious leaders have been men. Through exploring the teachings of fifteen women mystics – each with her own approach to what she calls 'the truth that goes beyond the ordinary' – Anne Bancroft gives a rare, cohesive and fascinating insight into the diversity of female approaches to mysticism.

Dynamics of the Unconscious: Seminars in Psychological Astrology Volume II   Liz Greene and Howard Sasportas

The authors of *The Development of the Personality* team up again to show how the dynamics of depth psychology interact with your birth chart. They shed new light on the psychology and astrology of aggression and depression – the darker elements of the adult personality that we must confront if we are to grow to find the wisdom within.

The Myth of Eternal Return: Cosmos and History   Mircea Eliade

'A luminous, profound, and extremely stimulating work . . . Eliade's thesis is that ancient man envisaged events not as constituting a linear, progressive history, but simply as so many creative repetitions of primordial archetypes . . . This is an essay which everyone interested in the history of religion and in the mentality of ancient man will have to read. It is difficult to speak too highly of it' – Theodore H. Gaster in *Review of Religion*.

Karma and Destiny in the I Ching   Guy Damian-Knight

This entirely original approach to the *I Ching*, achieved through mathematical rearrangement of the hexagrams, offers a new, more precise tool for self-understanding. Simple to use and yet profound, it gives the ancient Chinese classic a thoroughly contemporary relevance.

ARKANA – NEW-AGE BOOKS FOR MIND, BODY AND SPIRIT

A selection of titles already published or in preparation

A Course in Miracles: The Course, Workbook for Students and Manual for Teachers

Hailed as 'one of the most remarkable systems of spiritual truth available today', *A Course in Miracles* is a self-study course designed to shift our perceptions, heal our minds and change our behaviour, teaching us to experience miracles – 'natural expressions of love' – rather than problems generated by fear in our lives.

Medicine Woman: A Novel Lynn Andrews

The intriguing story of a white woman's journey of self-discovery among the Heyoka Indians – from the comforts of civilisation to the wilds of Canada. Apprenticed to a medicine woman, she learns tribal wisdom and mysticism – and above all the power of her own womanhood.

Arthur and the Sovereignty of Britain: Goddess and Tradition in the Mabinogion Caitlín Matthews

Rich in legend and the primitive magic of the Celtic Otherworld, the stories of the *Mabinogion* heralded the first flowering of European literature and became the source of Arthurian legend. Caitlín Matthews illuminates these stories, shedding light on Sovereignty, the Goddess of the Land and the spiritual principle of the Feminine.

Shamanism: Archaic Techniques of Ecstasy Mircea Eliade

Throughout Siberia and Central Asia, religious life traditionally centres around the figure of the shaman: magician and medicine man, healer and miracle-doer, priest and poet.

'Has become the standard work on the subject and justifies its claim to be the first book to study the phenomenon over a wide field and in a properly religious context' – *The Times Literary Supplement*

ARKANA – NEW-AGE BOOKS FOR MIND, BODY AND SPIRIT

A selection of titles already published or in preparation

The I Ching and You Diana ffarington Hook

A clear, accessible, step-by-step guide to the *I Ching* – the classic book of Chinese wisdom. Ideal for the reader seeking a quick guide to its fundamental principles, and the often highly subtle shades of meaning of its eight trigrams and sixty-four hexagrams.

A History of Yoga Vivian Worthington

The first of its kind, *A History of Yoga* chronicles the uplifting teachings of this ancient art in its many guises: at its most simple a beneficial exercise; at its purest an all-embracing quest for the union of body and mind.

Tao Te Ching The Richard Wilhelm Edition

Encompassing philosophical speculation and mystical reflection, the *Tao Te Ching* has been translated more often than any other book except the Bible, and more analysed than any other Chinese classic. Richard Wilhelm's acclaimed 1910 translation is here made available in English.

The Book of the Dead E. A. Wallis Budge

Intended to give the deceased immortality, the Ancient Egyptian *Book of the Dead* was a vital piece of 'luggage' on the soul's journey to the other world, providing for every need: victory over enemies, the procurement of friendship and – ultimately – entry into the kingdom of Osiris.

Yoga: Immortality and Freedom Mircea Eliade

Eliade's excellent volume explores the tradition of yoga with exceptional directness and detail.

'One of the most important and exhaustive single-volume studies of the major ascetic techniques of India and their history yet to appear in English' – *San Francisco Chronicle*